Cook Once a Week

Why We Love to Cook Once a Week

"Cook once a week? It almost sounds too good to be true! But Theresa Albert-Ratchford comes through for us time-pressed moms by showing us how we can spend less time in the kitchen and still manage to get healthy, kid-friendly meals on the dinner table. This is the ultimate cookbook for today's busy mom."

– Ann Douglas,
author of *The Mother of All Parenting Books*

"At last. A simple approach to preparing healthy and delicious family meals that are trans-fat free and bursting with the goodness of whole grains and colourful, flavourful vegetables that your kids will enjoy."

– Aileen Burford-Mason, Ph.D.,
immunologist/nutritional consultant

THERESA ALBERT-RATCHFORD

Cook Once a Week

Eat Well Every Day

HarperCollins*Publishers*Ltd

Dedicated to Guy and Jameson. From my first disaster, Jerk Tofu, through breast milk, baby food and Red River Cereal, all the way to Sushi for fireside supper—both of you have tried every bite, gave honest opinions and gave me the courage to go on.

Cook Once a Week
© 2005 by Thyme for Supper. All rights reserved.

Published by HarperCollins Publishers Ltd

First edition

HarperCollins books may be purchased for educational, business, or sales promotional use through our Special Markets Department.

HarperCollins Publishers Ltd
2 Bloor Street East, 20th Floor
Toronto, Ontario, Canada
M4W 1A8

www.harpercollins.ca

Photography by Hal Roth Photography Inc.
Food styling by Rosemarie Superville.

Library and Archives Canada Cataloguing in Publication

Albert-Ratchford, Theresa
Cook once a week : eat well every day /
Theresa Albert-Ratchford. – 1st ed.

ISBN 0-00-639510-4

1. Make-ahead cookery. I. Title.

TX652.A42 2004   641.5'55   C2004-905842-8

RRD 9 8 7 6 5 4 3 2 1

Printed and bound in the United States
Set in Akzidenz Grotesk

Contents

Introduction

Here's the secret to a meal planning system that will save you hours thinking about meals, grocery shopping and the kitchen. *Cook Once a Week* simplifies things by providing you with a weekly meal plan of surefire family pleasers. Most recipes are designed to be successfully doubled and the balance frozen for future use. Suggestions for making leftovers into brand-new meals (these are the Grab and Go part of the recipes) are included to stretch three cooked meals into five—one for every night of the workweek. The best part of the process is that each weekly plan is designed to be cooked all in one afternoon. Using no more than three hours on a Sunday, you can prepare not only that night's dinner but also the meals for the rest of the week. The economy of motion never looked so good. The idea is to get as much done as possible. If you have to be in the kitchen anyway, why not let it be the *only time* you lift or clean a pot all week!

All of your nutritional wishes have been considered. *Cook Once a Week* has few trans fats, has lower starch and carbs (we use whole grains) and keeps healthy fats in healthy proportions.

Cook Once a Week is designed not only to simplify and make meals healthful but also to reduce the cost of doing so. Buying only what you need reduces the feeling-guilty cycle of buying with the best of intentions, letting things rot then throwing them away. Our shopping lists include everything you need to get the job done (deliciously!) and nothing more. This is a much smarter way to shop.

We know that today's busy schedules have you at home for supper about three nights per workweek and the rest are grab as you can, so we have planned for exactly that with a little for leftovers. A quick, nourishing lunch or two is just one of the bonuses of our system. Everything is based on a family of four, which is a round number, so you can scale up or down as needed. Kids under eight usually eat half portions, kids between the ages of eight and 12 can count as about three-quarter portions, and kids over 12 are anybody's guess from zero to two portions. You'll have to figure out the adolescent stomach as you go along—just like their clothes and music.

We have included an entire chapter of recipes for kids to make with you (see Bonus Kids Week). If you've got little ones, we suggest that this meal plan be your first foray into your new system for two reasons: the meals are utterly kid friendly and the recipes are the easiest of them all! Some families will use the Bonus Kids Week over and over again, venturing only into the other chapters when they have company or host a big family dinner. For fussy eaters, perhaps your best bet is to make these kids' meals and freeze everything in single-serving sizes. Kids can microwave them *only after they have tried the rest of what is put on the table*. No hassling or arguing; simply suggest that they get one of the meals that *they* made and microwave it. As long as your microwave oven is within reach, any child over three can do this—with supervision.

Our experience with kids tells us that they are much more likely to eat something that they have invested in, and we do suggest that the Sunday cook-a-thon include them as soon as they can hold a knife—whether you're making the Bonus Week meals or any others. You can start them around age two with a plastic "lettuce knife" and let them cut up salad greens, then graduate to a serrated bread knife, which is easier to handle and harder to cut oneself with. By age three, they can handle a small paring knife if watched and guided well. I have taught many six-, seven- and eight-year-olds to use a ten-inch chef's knife safely as long as they are the kind of kid who can keep their eye on the job.

How to use this book

Each week has a work schedule that outlines how you are going to accomplish a week's worth of healthy cooking in three or so hours. Getting everything prepared on Sunday so that cooking the evening meal on any day later in the week is a simple, one-step process is the foundation of this book. The work schedule will help you plan the preparations, and the end result on a busy week night will be almost like stopping for take-out on the way home and warming it up in your own oven. Except cheaper, healthier and yummier!

Here's how to get going:

- When starting a meal plan, set out all recipe ingredients in groups around the kitchen. You don't need any special equipment or a large space by any means. The idea is that you use your space well: one side of the sink for veggies, one side for raw meat; one side of your stove for cooking one dish and the other for cooking the second dish or prepping something else.
- The recipes are in order of what you start first so you can read each week's recipes from beginning to end and just keep moving until all of your ingredients are off the counter and in the pots. Once you get going, it will become clear what needs to happen next. For instance, when you hit a point in the first recipe that says "simmer for 20 minutes" you can move on to the next recipe and get it started. By having "stations" around the stove, you can see what goes where and you won't have to keep checking the recipe and running to the fridge. Your first attempt will be the clumsiest but don't give up! Like anything, the routine will become, well, routine. Each week is designed to ease you further into the process, starting with the simplest and moving to the more complex.
- A note about garbage: always keep a large bowl for discards at the back of your

counter space when working. This eliminates the unnecessary steps to your waste or compost bin over and over again. Emptying one container at the end of the cooking session is much more hygienic and efficient than making several dozen trips to the trash. Place one bowl next to your stove and one next to your sink directly in front of you.

- Assess your storage needs. If you want to store your soups in single-serving sizes because your family eats at different times, then please do so. If you are the set-the-casserole-on-the-table kind of household then be sure to freeze it all in one container. The reheating instructions are intended to be flexible and you can adjust the reheating times up or down depending on your needs. It is always better to freeze in shallow containers because the freezing process happens more quickly, keeping food fresher, and the reheating process is faster.

As you go along, you will find that you always have one or two dishes in the freezer for quick meals. When you find that a dish is a hit with the whole family, be sure to double it next time you make it and freeze for future use.

We have provided you with grocery lists for each week. Each list has all of the ingredients that you need for that week, including the Grab and Go options (usually for four servings). Once you are sure which meals will go over with everyone (and we have plenty of variation ideas for the fussiest members) you can photocopy the list to increase the amount of each ingredient as needed to double or triple a recipe. Or visit www.cookonceaweek.ca. You will find all the shopping lists there for you in downloadable form.

When you have a complete list of all that you need for the weekly plan (including your up-sizing, if necessary), you can photocopy this plan multiple times so you can use it over again throughout the season. Try keeping a binder with these shopping lists and tracking your grocery bills. Family life being the circus that it is, we are sure the other copies will get misplaced, splattered upon or chewed by the dog. Do yourself a favour and keep this copy. Don't lose sight of this page of crucial information!

At the end of each week there is a blank page, ready to be filled with your notes. What did your kids like best? Did you change up some spicing, increase serving sizes? Write it down so you won't forget.

All weeks are designed to cost approximately $75 for the foundation of the meals, assuming that you have a few of the staples on hand. If you choose to use the Grab and Go recipes to help you with quick solutions for leftovers, then you can assume the groceries will cost another $25. Storage containers and sealable freezer bags will cost extra but can be reused often.

Good luck and enjoy all the free time that *Cook Once a Week* will give you.

Getting organized

One of the things I do in the coaching role of my job is to show people how to get through that planning, shopping and cooking process more efficiently. I am amazed at how many people try to skip that step of planning. Then they are, in turn, amazed at how much food rots in their fridge. The process is detailed, but here are my best tips.

Shopping

- Find out which day your market gets produce deliveries and shop on those days. The best idea is to shop and cook on the same day so you can skip the step of putting things away!
- Always shop at the same store because you will get to know what they carry and where to find it quickly.
- Try to shop early in the day or later in the evening, when stores are quieter.
- Take your list with you. Do not try to "remember" at the store.
- When shopping, be sure to gather all items from the perimeter of the store first. All fresh items will be found there, and you'll need only a very few minutes in specific aisles to gather canned or packaged goods.
- Take extra produce bags and use them for meat but skip them for most veggies because they are another unnecessary step.
- Using a bin or a box instead of grocery bags saves time at the store and at home, not to mention the environmental bonus. Just pack your own bins and put similar things in one bin–pantry items, fresh meat with dairy and vegetables, canned goods. When you get home, it will be easy to assign one person to the cupboard and one to the fridge for unpacking duties.
- Store ingredients when possible in their recipe grouping. Keeping all of the vegetables for a certain soup in one bag or corner makes a quicker start.
- If you are lucky enough to live in an urban centre with online shopping and delivery, be sure to save your list in their system so you only have to shop once and your precious list will be there to use again.

Cooking

- Take out all required pots and bowls to start.
- Clean and chop all veggies for all recipes at once so you are not running from the sink to the stove.
- Fry all onions (or common ingredients such as celery, peppers, etc.) required in one pan then separate them into pots as needed.

- Get one recipe under control or to the "simmer for . . ." stage before moving on to the next.
- If you modify a recipe, make notes so you will be able make the same changes each time.

Storing

- Choose shallow, long storage containers if possible. They will cool and freeze more efficiently, preserving vitamins and improving food safety; they will also thaw and reheat faster.
- Move a finished product from the hot to the cold stage as quickly as possible. Do not cool on the counter. It is safer to put items in the fridge away from perishables such as meat and milk.
- Label items with tape and a permanent marker and include the date. You might remember, but chances are you won't. I don't and I do this for a living. The time used solving mysteries from your freezer is better spent just about anywhere else.

Breakfast

Some of the most stressful moments in any family household are during the morning hours. Our picture of the 1950s mom in the kitchen calling the boys to a breakfast of bacon and eggs with toast and juice seems almost absurd in today's harried life. But there are ways to make breakfast go smoothly and to take the pressure off. A box of cereal is not really the answer as it provides mostly carbohydrates and very little protein. The grumbly tummy will be looking for more sugar by recess. A few hints on breakfast are all you need because it is the most often repeated meal of the week. You would not dream of serving the same pizza five days in a row, but often today's breakfast looks just like yesterday's.

The secret is in the planning. When you have time on the weekend to prepare a few things, why not make a few more and freeze them for the week?

BREAKFAST PLAN 1: FRENCH TOAST

French toast is a chameleon with protein, omega-3 fatty acids, whole grains, calcium and then some. It has many faces and is great to make ahead and freeze to be microwaved during the weekday rush.

Basic French Toast: Stir together 1 egg, 2 tbsp (25 mL) milk, 1/2 tsp (2 mL) sugar, 1/2 tsp (2 mL) cinnamon for each slice of whole wheat bread. Scale up per person. (Add extra bread for cooking now to freeze for the week.) Soak bread in the egg mixture for a few minutes. Fry in a nonstick pan sprayed with cooking spray over medium heat until brown; flip and brown the other side (about 2 minutes per side). Eat now, or cool and freeze.

VARIATIONS

Buttermilk French Toast: Use low-fat buttermilk instead of milk for a creamier texture. The nutrients are the same but the fluffier texture is sometimes more appealing.

Juicy French Toast: Substitute orange, apple, pineapple or any favourite juice for the milk in the main recipe.

English Muffin or Bagel French Toast: Substitute any type of bread for a change.

Shapes Toast: Allow kids to use cookie cutters to shape their toast any way they like. Try to use large cutters to reduce waste. Don't throw away the crusts: just eat them yourself.

Stuffed French Toast: Ham and cheese sandwiches can be turned into Croque Monsieurs by dipping in egg mixture and frying. Any of your favourite lunch fillings work.

Apple Cheesecake French Toast: Put cream cheese and apple slices between two pieces of hot, cooked French toast with a little sprinkle of cinnamon.

TOPPINGS

Of course maple syrup is called for but you can reduce its use by providing other toppings. Fruit is always at the top of the list for adding vitamins and fibre into each meal.

Frozen Blueberry Compote: Bring 2 tbsp (25 mL) each water and granulated sugar to boil and dissolve. Add 1 cup (250 mL) frozen blueberries and bring to boil; simmer for 5 minutes. Store in fridge up to 2 weeks.

Frozen Strawberry Compote: Bring 2 tbsp (25 mL) each water and sugar to boil and dissolve. Add 1 cup (250 mL) frozen strawberries and bring to boil; simmer for 5 minutes. Store in fridge up to 2 weeks.

Apple Compote: This is great for those apples that are going a little soft. Keep the skins on if you can get away with it. Just scrub and rinse well and chop off bruised bits. Bring 2 tbsp (25 mL) each water and sugar to boil and dissolve. Add 1 cup (250 mL) chopped apples and 1 tsp (5 mL) cinnamon and bring to boil; simmer for 5 minutes. Store in fridge up to 2 weeks.

BREAKFAST PLAN 2: DESSERT FOR BREAKFAST

One of the problems with breakfast is its reputation. It can be a boring meal that is pressure filled since it truly is the foundation of the day. Breaking fast is important for the growing (or groaning) brain that has used up all of its fuel overnight and just can't get into gear without something to burn. To take the pressure off, why not let breakfast be a dessert meal? You can feel good about serving any one of our desserts for breakfast (see recipes on pages 120 to 133). They are all designed with nutrition in mind and have healthy doses of protein, fruits and vegetables.

BREAKFAST PLAN 3: SHAKE IT UP

Think of your blender as your best friend. Let kids fill it the night before to refrigerate with any combination of the ingredients below. Pick one from each category and simply blend them together in the morning. Each pitcher will serve two to three people.

Liquid (2 cups/500 mL)	Fruit	Protein	Add Ins
vanilla soy milk	1 banana	2 tbsp (30 mL) almond butter	1 tsp (5 mL) ground flaxseed
chocolate soy milk	1/2 cup (125 mL) frozen raspberries	1/2 cup (125 mL) silken tofu	1 tsp (5 mL) cinnamon
milk	1/2 cup (125 mL) frozen blueberries	2 tbsp (30 mL) peanut butter	1 tsp (5 mL) vanilla
orange juice	1/2 cup (125 mL) applesauce	1 tsp (5 mL) wheat germ	

BREAKFAST PLAN 4: WHATEVER WORKS

There are a few of us who don't like breakfast at all and would prefer lunch food. Our culture is unique in its reliance on grains and specific breakfast meals. Many cultures simply have variations of the other meals in the morning hours. For instance, in Japan you would have rice, miso soup and some kind of fish; in Mexico you would not be surprised to see beans on your plate. If your family has a favourite food, don't balk at reheating it for breakfast. It can be fun to have soup or chili at this meal once in a while. If they ask for it, break the rules and give it to them.

Lunch

Lunch stumps. If you are forced to pack a lunch to send to school then you have to walk the line between sending something familiar so your kids don't get teased and sending something nutritious. If you spend any time at all in most school lunch rooms you will see more packaged foods than homemade lunches. You will also see the dessert eaten first, the fruit thrown into the garbage and more talking than eating going on. If your children are sent to school with a good breakfast, you can breathe easily knowing that they will make it through the day without starving, so there is no need to go to the lowest common denominator to get them to "eat something, anything!" Liquid is most important here. A good drink will keep their bodies from becoming dehydrated and that is just as important as lunch. The trick here, then, is a glass of milk (preferably purchased from school so you don't have to stock and transport it) and something interesting enough for them to nibble.

If milk is not available at school then invest in a few small containers that you can pour milk into and partially freeze so it stays cold. Nothing turns you off milk faster than a big gulp of sour milk. A tiny packet of chocolate powder is not the end of the world and it is a better option than buying the chocolate milk itself. Although I am dead against the caffeine in cocoa being fed to kids, some kids simply won't drink white milk, and at least you can control the amount by packaging a teaspoon of chocolate milk powder mixed with a teaspoon of instant dry powdered milk to boost the calcium. Letting the kids add it themselves adds to the fun.

VEGGIE STRATEGIES

The big hurdle is vegetables. Being realistic about what our kids will eat out of our sight means making the food as attractive as possible and keeping portions small. Do not send what you know they will waste. Letting them see your commitment to vegetables sets up a lifelong brainwashing, in a good way. Invest in a crinkle cutter so your carrot sticks look all wiggly and your celery stuffed with cream cheese has a wavy appearance. Dips are a good idea, too. Pick up some tiny containers that you can fill with salsa or guacamole at best or bottled dressing at worst. Hey, whatever gets it in. A few vegetables dipped into Very Cheesy Yogurt Dip (1 cup/250 mL yogurt mixed with 1/2 cup/125 mL shredded Cheddar cheese and 1 tsp/5 mL mayonnaise) and a handful of whole grain, trans fat free crackers make for a decent lunch. For extra vegetables, take a look at our recipe for Krispy Kale (page 44). If it is packed in a hard container, it will travel well, and the similarity to potato chips makes it acceptable to younger tongues.

MUFFINS

Sometimes getting vegetables into a child means hiding them, and that means baking. Sweet Potato Muffins (page 122) or Zucchini Muffins (page 123) are good disguises that contain a whole grain, some vegetables and some protein from the eggs. Even one of these and a glass of milk is a balanced meal.

MEAT AND OTHER PROTEINS

Another thing that you want in that lunch box is some protein. Our kids, being the carbohydrate hounds that they are, most often prefer bread with something on it, but even they get bored of that so try some of these ideas:

Meat "Fries": Slice a few pieces of meat from Sunday dinner into French-fry shapes and send some ketchup or mustard for them to dip.

Lunch Rolls: These are simply sliced meats rolled around a slice of apple or melon and stuck with a toothpick. Try prosciutto or turkey meat rather than ham or bologna. Prosciutto is dry cured without nitrites, and turkey is leaner than the other two.

Soups, Stews, Pasta: The vacuum bottle needs to make a comeback. Send any of the soups or stews that the kids like from your supper meals. Pasta is great too. Fresh spinach tortellini has fibre and folic acid in it and if you buy the fresh product made with whole eggs, you are getting extra protein. It is a nice treat, especially if you send some tomato sauce as a dip.

Wieners: These can go in a vacuum bottle for a good surprise. Try veggie wieners early in life and the kids will like them more than the beef kind, but even chicken is a leaner choice than beef. Be sure to boil them beforehand and place in a vacuum bottle to keep them at a safe temperature until lunch. Wrap favourite toppings in snack size resealable containers to go along with the bun.

Grab and Go: Many of our dinner meals have grab-and-go ideas that you can wrap up in a whole wheat tortilla and send along for lunch. Wraps are great because they use much less bread to get the job done, and whole wheat or spinach wraps are more nutritious bite for bite than the plain variety. Be sure to check the label because some wraps do contain partially hydrogenated shortening, which contains trans fatty acids.

Lunch-ables: There are some great containers that have little compartments so you can make your own lunch pack. How about a Make-Your-Own Pizza with mini whole wheat pitas in one compartment, tomato sauce in another and shredded cheese in the third? A few slices of meat can go into another container and the kids can build the pizza at school.

WEEK 1

This starts you off with a truly simple, no-fail week. These recipes are very familiar yet have simple adjustments to make them healthier and easier. The Better Spaghetti Sauce recipe is my secret weapon. Not a week goes by that I don't use some version of this, which is always in my freezer. Our family loves its sweetness, which is provided by the vegetables (but don't tell them that!). If I don't have ground beef, I use ground chicken. If I have vegetarians over I use Veggie Ground Round. I serve it in every combination imaginable: over pasta, in wraps, as a pizza topping or just out of the microwave with a spoon (while I take a four-minute lunch break like every other mother I know).

I was demonstrating the flexibility of this recipe once on a television program while my husband and daughter watched from home—she was about eight years old. As I was grating onion and various other "gross" vegetables into the sauce, he had to hold back laughter while she looked on in horror. "No way, she puts that in it? Ewwww, I am never eating spaghetti again!" she said. Her resolve only lasted a few hours when she figured out that it tasted good anyway.

Basics But Better

Better Spaghetti Sauce

*Roasted Chicken to Please Everybody
(with roasted carrots, potatoes and rutabaga)

Pork Roast Dijon

Steamed Snow Peas

WORK SCHEDULE

1 Start spaghetti sauce first, as it needs to simmer while you prepare the remaining recipes. Half of this can be stored in the fridge to use this week and the other half should be frozen in single serving sizes for up to 4 weeks.

2 Prepare veggies for the chicken dish and lay on baking sheet.

3 Rinse the chicken, pat dry with paper towel and place in its roasting pan; cover with plastic wrap and refrigerate.

4 Prepare pork and place in resealable freezer bag in freezer.

5 Sweet potatoes can be stored in a cool dry cupboard and snow peas in the fridge for the night that you are serving Pork Roast Dijon.

6 Prepare snow peas only when you are ready to serve the Pork Roast Dijon dinner.

*Serve it tonight.

Better Spaghetti Sauce

SERVES
4+4

PREPARATION TIME
30 MINUTES

This sauce recipe rinses away much of the saturated fat and loads up on hidden vegetables, which virtually disappear during the cooking process. It contains four to five times as much vegetable as meat, a healthy ratio.

Stir the ground flaxseed into the sauce at the end of cooking to maintain all of the "good fats." This invisible seed adds fibre. Do not use the seed whole because our bodies cannot break down the hull to digest all of the goodness.

Frozen mashed squash is not always available but cubed fresh or frozen squash is a good substitute. Simply add it and mash with a fork as it cooks and softens.

Cook sauce today and have options all week.

1 lb (500 g) extra-lean ground beef
1 tsp (5 mL) canola oil
1 onion, grated
2 carrots, grated
1 sweet green pepper, seeded, cored and grated

3 cloves garlic, minced
1 tbsp (15 mL) Italian herb seasoning
1 tsp (5 mL) fennel seed (optional)
2 cups (500 mL) frozen mashed squash

1 can (26 oz/796 mL) tomato sauce
1 can (5 1/2 oz/156 mL) tomato paste
1 cup (250 mL) red wine
1/4 cup (50 mL) ground flaxseed

• In skillet, brown meat; place meat in a strainer in sink. Run under hot water to drain as much of the fat as possible. Set aside.

• In large saucepan, heat oil; cook onion, carrots and green pepper until softened. Add cooked ground beef. Stir in garlic and Italian seasoning. Add fennel seed (if using).

• Add squash and heat through. Add tomato sauce, tomato paste and wine. Simmer for at least 20 minutes or for up to 1 1/2 hours. Stir in ground flaxseed.

Grab and Go 1

Beef Burritos: Wrap any leftover sauce in whole wheat tortillas and then individually in plastic wrap. For a quick weeknight meal, microwave for 1 to 2 minutes per wrap.

Grab and Go 2

Better Nachos: Freeze sauce in 1/2 cup (125 mL) sizes. Reheat in microwave. Place a package of low-salt corn chips on a plate, top with warmed sauce then shredded Cheddar cheese. Broil for 1 to 2 minutes to melt cheese and you have a quickie nacho meal to serve with carrot and celery sticks.

Roasted Chicken to Please Everybody

Removing the kids' portions before you add the extra garlic and herb flavourings ensures that everyone gets what they want.

2 red potatoes	2 tbsp (30 mL) garlic oil	1/4 cup (50 mL) white wine
3 carrots	1 chicken (3 to 4 lb/1.5 to	Salt and pepper to taste
1 small rutabaga	2 kg), backbone removed	1 sprig fresh tarragon
1 onion	1 head garlic	

- Wash and scrub potatoes and carrots but do not peel; chop into loonie-sized pieces. Peel and cube rutabaga into dime-sized pieces. Quarter onion and then peel and discard skin.
- Spread on foil-lined baking sheet; drizzle with half of the garlic oil.
- Rinse chicken under cold running water; pat dry with paper towel. Place in shallow roasting pan, skin side up. Break head of garlic in half; place unpeeled under chicken. Press down on chicken to flatten slightly. Mix wine, remaining oil, salt and pepper; drizzle over chicken. Cover with plastic wrap and refrigerate for up to 24 hours.
- Roast chicken and vegetables in 350°F (180°C) oven for 1 1/2 hours or until meat thermometer registers 185°F (85°C) and juices run clear when chicken is pierced and vegetables are tender.
- Carve and remove pieces for children from portion of chicken that they like. Return remaining adult pieces to roasting pan.
- Remove garlic halves and squeeze into bowl. Coarsely chop tarragon leaves and mix into garlic. If desired, remove as much chicken skin as possible to reduce calories and fat. Using fork, smear paste onto chicken pieces for adults. Broil for 2 minutes. Serve with roasted vegetables.

Grab and Go 1
Chicken Salad Wrap: Chop remaining chicken and mix with 1 tbsp (15 mL) each plain yogurt and mayonnaise or just enough to moisten. Eat sandwiches or wraps within 3 days.

Grab and Go 2
Chopped Chicken Salad Suey: Leftover chicken can be chopped along with cooked root vegetables and tossed with 2 tbsp (30 mL) low-sodium soy sauce, 1 tsp (5 mL) Dijon mustard and 1/2 tsp (2 mL) toasted sesame oil. Serve on mixed greens for a great lunch salad. A few rice crackers can be crushed and sprinkled on top for low-fat croutons.

SERVES
4+2

PREPARATION TIME
15 MINUTES

Remove all leftover meat from bones and store in fridge up to 3 days or freeze up to 3 weeks. Carcass can be broken and boiled in 6 cups (1.5 L) water with 1 chopped onion (skin on for colour) to make stock or frozen for 3 weeks.

If you won't drink the remaining wine in the bottle, search for mini bottles. Many retailers carry a 300 mL size that will do for just a recipe or two. You could also use other alcohol here—the sherry left over from Christmas, the beer in the fridge, the grappa from that Mediterranean party.

Ask the butcher (even at the grocery store) to remove the backbone. This reduces the cooking time by eliminating the need to heat the empty chicken cavity. To remove the backbone yourself, grip the tail with paper towel and hold firmly while you slide a sharp knife up the back along one side of the spine, cutting away from you. You will reach some resistance when you get to the middle back but holding the bird upside down and pushing your knife downward toward the cutting board will give you the leverage needed.

Pork Roast Dijon

SERVES
4

PREPARATION TIME
10 MINUTES

Ground almonds boost the protein and good fat. They can be found in the baking section of the grocery store.

Serve with steamed snow peas.

1/3 cup (75 mL) ground
   almonds
1 cup (250 mL) white wine
   (approx)

3 tbsp (45 mL) Dijon mustard
1/2 tsp (2 mL) pepper
2 lb (1 kg) rolled boneless
   pork centre loin roast

4 small sweet potatoes,
   scrubbed
1 tsp (5 mL) olive oil
Salt and pepper to taste

- In large resealable plastic bag, mix almonds, wine, mustard and pepper. Add roast and smear almond mixture all over meat. (Refrigerate for up to 3 days. Or freeze for up to 3 weeks; thaw in refrigerator for 24 to 48 hours.)

- Cut sweet potatoes into 8 wedges each. Place in large resealable plastic bag along with oil, salt and pepper; shake to coat. (Refrigerate for up to 48 hours.)

- Arrange potatoes in single layer on foil-covered baking sheet. Place roast and as much almond mixture as possible, fat side up, in shallow roasting pan. Roast potatoes on upper rack and pork on lower rack of 375°F (190°C) oven for 60 to 90 minutes or until meat thermometer reaches 160°F (70°C), adding 1/4 cup (50 mL) more wine if pan starts to burn.

Grab and Go:

Pork and Spinach Roll-Up: Even a little bit of pork is great chopped and mixed with balsamic vinaigrette then rolled into burrito wraps with some baby spinach. These can be refrigerated up to 24 hours and served cold.

Steamed Snow Peas

2 cups (500 mL) fresh snow pea pods	1 tbsp (15 mL) white wine 1 tsp (5 mL) granulated sugar	Salt and pepper to taste

PREPARATION TIME
3 MINUTES

- Rinse snow peas under cold water and place in large microwaveable bowl; sprinkle with wine, sugar, salt and pepper. (Can be covered with plastic wrap and refrigerated up to 24 hours.)
- Microwave, covered, on high for 2 to 4 minutes or until bright green and crisp-tender.

Week 1 Shopping List

YOU NEED:

*Whole wheat tortillas (6)
*Cheddar cheese (1 lb/500 g)
*Plain yogurt (1 tbsp/15 mL)
Extra-lean ground beef (1 lb/500 g)
Chicken (3 to 4 lb/1.5 to 2 kg), backbone removed
Rolled boneless pork roast (2 lb/1 kg)
Red potatoes (2)
Green pepper (1)
Sweet potatoes (4 small)
Rutabaga (1 small)
Fresh tarragon (1 bunch)
Garlic (2 heads)
Snow pea pods (2 cups/500 mL)
Carrots (5)
Lemon juice (1 tsp/5 mL)
Onions (2)
*Baby spinach (1 pkg, 10 oz/300 g)
Frozen mashed squash (1 pkg, 1 lb/ 400 g)

CHECK YOUR PANTRY FOR:

Red wine (1 cup/250 mL)
White wine (1 1/4 cups/300 mL + 1 tbsp/15 mL)
Dijon mustard (3 tbsp/45 mL + 1 tsp/5 mL)
Garlic oil (2 tbsp/30 mL)
Ground flaxseed (1/4 cup/50 mL)
Whole wheat pasta (1 pkg, 2 lb/900 g)
Ground almonds (1/3 cup/75 mL)
Fennel seed (1 tsp/5 mL)
Italian herb seasoning (1 tbsp/15 mL)
Tomato paste (1 can, 5 1/2 oz/156 mL)
Tomato sauce (1 can, 26 oz/796 mL)
*Low-salt corn chips (1 pkg)
*Light mayonnaise (1 tbsp/15 mL)
*Low-sodium soy sauce (2 tbsp/30 mL)
*Toasted sesame oil (1/2 tsp/2 mL)
*Balsamic vinaigrette (1 tbsp/15 mL)
Canola oil (1 tsp/5 mL)
Olive oil (1 tsp/5 mL)
Granulated sugar (1 tsp/5 mL)

*grab and go items

Notes

WEEK 2

From time to time in our neighbourhood, usually right around dinnertime, come the jingly tinkles of the ice-cream truck. Once I overheard a slightly exasperated father calmly tell his three-year-old, "Yes, son, that is the vegetable truck." While my husband and I chuckled at his ingenuity at first, some uneasiness about this approach later set in. What worries me is the unspoken lesson: vegetables are yucky and you wouldn't want them. Kids these days, we are told, are overwhelmed with stress and eat more bad food much earlier than we ever did. They therefore need the superhero powers that only vegetables can give them. We are doing them a huge favour when we expose them to as many vegetables as possible. Don't give up. Try raw, cooked and even frozen. Why can't frozen broccoli be a "tree popsicle"? Whatever works! Kids need to see a new food many times before they will try it, and making vegetables a positive part of their lives is a good first step.

Entertaining the Whole Fam Damily

Grilled Vegetable Soup

Black Bean Nachos

✳Sunday Ham with Potatoes

Veggie Platter

WORK SCHEDULE

1　Start grilled veggies for soup. When done, pull out 2 to 3 cups (500 to 750 mL) to serve as a side dish for tonight's dinner. Complete soup for freezing.

2　Complete Black Bean Nachos to freeze.

3　Prepare ham and scrub potatoes. Set in fridge until ready to cook for tonight's supper.

4　Chop veggies for platter to serve as an appetizer today or store in fridge in resealable plastic bag with a piece of paper towel and they will last at least 3 days to give you a head start for the week.

✳Serve it tonight.

Grilled Vegetable Soup

SERVES
8

PREPARATION TIME
20 MINUTES

Serve this soup, topped with grated Parmesan, with whole grain bread and Cheddar cheese.

1 head garlic	3 sweet red peppers	3 cups (750 mL) frozen corn
10 plum tomatoes	2 sweet green peppers	10 cups (2.5 L) chicken stock
4 zucchini	1 sweet onion	2 tbsp (30 mL) pesto sauce

Tips

Pesto sauce is a wonderful ingredient that adds flavour to everything. Spread it on frozen pizza or stir it into soups. Try it on a bagel with cream cheese or toss some with leftover potatoes and make a potato salad.

As you chop the veggies for this recipe, freeze the trimmings to make soup stock for Sunday Ham Soup (page 44).

Even if the kids eat only the soup broth with some whole grain bread and cheese, they are still getting protein, calcium and carbohydrate. Reduce the amount of cheese for a calorie-restricted diet.

Using frozen chicken stock, the sodium count is minimal. Using canned stock, the sodium per serving is a whopping 3179 mg.

- Wrap garlic in foil; place in oven while vegetables broil.
- Slice tomatoes thickly. Chop zucchini and red and green peppers into bite-sized pieces. Spread on foil-covered baking sheets. Broil, in batches and stirring halfway through, 4 inches (10 cm) from heat until starting to brown, 15 to 20 minutes.
- Coarsely chop onion; spread with corn on separate baking sheet. Broil for 10 to 15 minutes until niblets are brown, watching carefully to prevent burning.
- Remove 2 to 3 cups (500 to 750 mL) of veggies and arrange on platter for tonight; cover and refrigerate until ready to serve with ham.
- In large pot, bring stock to simmer. Add remaining broiled vegetables and pesto sauce; cook for 5 minutes on low heat. Let cool. Turn off broiler but leave garlic in oven until softened; squeeze into soup.
- Freeze in single or multiple portions up to 4 weeks; to reheat, warm on stovetop in pot, stirring gently, or microwave for 2 to 10 minutes.

Grab and Go

Roasted Veggie Frittata: Reserve some favourite grilled veggies to toss into a frittata. With a fork, mix 8 eggs with 1/4 cup (50 mL) milk. Preheat oven to 450°F (230°C). In skillet, heat 1 tbsp (15 mL) canola oil over medium-high heat; add eggs and cook for 2 minutes until starting to bubble. Add roasted vegetables and some shredded cheese; place in oven, uncovered, until heated through, 8 to 10 minutes.

Black Bean Nachos

Here's a fast, colourful meal for a busy weeknight. To keep calories and fat low, limit cheese and corn chips.

Half sweet onion, chopped
1 tbsp (15 mL) olive oil
1 cup (250 mL) canned tomatoes, chopped
1 1/2 cups (375 mL) frozen
   corn

1 can (19 oz/540 mL) black
   beans, drained and rinsed
2 tbsp (30 mL) lime juice
1 tbsp (15 mL) chili powder
1 tsp (5 mL) dried oregano
8 oz (250 g) Cheddar cheese,
   shredded

1 pkg (10 oz/300 g) frozen
   chopped spinach, thawed
   and squeezed dry
2 cups (500 mL) salsa
1 pkg (350 g) low-fat tortilla
   chips

- In saucepan, sauté onion in oil for about 8 minutes, covered, until very soft. Stir in tomatoes, corn, black beans, lime juice, chili powder and oregano; cook 5 minutes to heat through.
- Spoon into 8-inch (2 L) casserole dish; sprinkle with half of the Cheddar. Arrange spinach over top. Spoon on half of the salsa. (Can be covered and refrigerated for up to 3 days or frozen for 4 weeks.)
- Bake in 350°F (180°C) oven for 45 minutes. Arrange tortilla chips on ovenproof platter. Invort black bean mixture over chips; top with remaining Cheddar. Bake for 10 minutes. Serve with remaining salsa.

SERVES
4+3

PREPARATION TIME
15 MINUTES

Keep some chips aside so the kids can have salsa, chips and cheese for dinner if they are not keen on beans. Baby carrots and celery for dipping are all you need to balance this meal.

Grab and Go

Stuffed Mini Pitas: Cut a slit in the tops of 9 mini whole wheat pitas and stuff leftovers, chips and all, into pitas. Place 3 stuffed pitas in each of 3 resealable plastic bags and refrigerate up to 3 days. To serve, warm on plate in microwave for 1 minute. Top with Cheddar cheese and rezap to melt it. Serve with chunks of avocado and a mini dish of salsa.

Sunday Ham with Potatoes

SERVES
4+4

PREPARATION TIME
20 MINUTES

Whole cloves make great pot-
pourri. When your house is a little
stuffy from a combination of dogs
and kids, put a pot on the stove
containing 2 cups (500 mL)
water, 1/4 cup (50 mL) vinegar
and a handful of cloves. Simmer
for 10 to 60 minutes and your
home will smell great. Just watch
that the pot does not boil dry: top
up with water as needed.

Freeze bone and any scraps for
Sunday Ham Soup (page 44).

Remember ham is fully cooked
and you are just heating through
as well as flavouring the meat, so
reduce the temperature and
increase the cooking time or
alternatively increase the temperature up to 400°F (200°C) and
reduce time to 1 hour if it is more
convenient.

Serve tonight with a side dish of roasted veggies borrowed from the roasted vegetable
soup. Drizzle the vegetables with a little balsamic vinegar and olive oil.

3 tbsp (45 mL) whole cloves
9 lb (4 kg) cooked bone-in ham
1/4 cup (50 mL) warm water

1/4 cup (50 mL) honey mustard
1/4 cup (50 mL) balsamic
   vinegar

1/4 cup (50 mL) brown sugar
4 baking potatoes

- Poke cloves into ham in random pattern. Place ham in roasting pan. Mix warm water, mustard,
vinegar and brown sugar; pour over ham. Scrub potatoes; poke a few holes to let steam
escape so they don't burst.
- Bake ham and potatoes in 300°F (150°C) oven for up to 3 hours or until hot throughout and
potatoes are tender. Serve with pan juices.

Grab and Go

Sunday Ham Reprise: A second meal is only as far away as your foil. Fill large squares of foil with
3 or 4 slices each of ham; cover with any juices. Freeze in resealable plastic bags up to 3 weeks.
Bake on baking sheet along with 4 scrubbed sweet potatoes in 375°F (190°C) oven for 45 minutes to serve as a second meal. Microwave some frozen green beans just minutes before you
are ready to serve.

Veggie Platter

SERVES
4

Always put out a platter of veggies after school or just before supper. This is when kids are at their hungriest and are more likely to munch. Add some fruit once in a while and try fresh herbs; kids who won't touch salad will nibble on parsley or mint.

PREPARATION TIME
20 MINUTES

1 each sweet red and yellow pepper

1 head broccoli
1 head celery

2 cups (500 mL) fresh snow pea pods

• Seed, core and slice red and yellow peppers. Cut broccoli into florets. Cut broccoli stalks and celery into short lengths. Place in freezer bag along with snow peas. Add paper towel to wick away moisture, replacing when wet.

Week 2 Shopping List

YOU NEED:

*Whole wheat mini pitas (9)
Whole grain bread (1 large loaf)
Grated Parmesan cheese
   (1/3 cup/75 mL)
Cheddar cheese (1 lb/500 g)
*Eggs (8)
Milk (1/4 cup/50 mL)
Frozen corn (4 1/2 cups, 1125 mL)
*Frozen green beans (3 cups/750 mL)
Frozen chopped spinach
   (1 pkg, 10 oz/300 g)
Ham, bone in (9 lb/4 kg)
Plum tomatoes (10)
Red peppers (4)
Green peppers (2)
Yellow pepper (1)
Zucchini (4)
Baking potatoes (4)
*Sweet potatoes (4)
Sweet onions (2)
Garlic (1 head)
Celery (1 head)
Broccoli (1 head)
Snow peas (2 cups/500 mL)
Lime juice (2 tbsp/30 mL)
Low-fat tortilla chips (1 pkg, 350 g)

CHECK YOUR PANTRY FOR:

Brown sugar (1/4 cup/50 mL)
Black beans (1 can, 19 oz/540 mL)
Canned tomatoes (1 cup/250 mL)
Honey mustard (1/4 cup/50 mL)
Pesto sauce (2 tbsp/30 mL)
Olive oil (1 tbsp/15 mL)
*Canola oil (1 tbsp/15 mL)
Salsa (1 jar, 500 mL)
Chicken stock (10 cups/2.5 L)
Dried oregano (1 tsp/5 mL)
Chili powder (1tbsp/15 mL)
Whole cloves (3 tbsp/45 mL)
Balsamic vinegar (1/4 cup/50 mL)

*grab and go items

Notes

WEEK 3

While writing this cookbook, I had many clients, friends and colleagues offer to test my recipes and weekly plans. Although the individual recipes and meal plans work well for me when I'm cooking for clients, I wanted to be sure that the plans work for the "mom on the street." I outlined very loosely what I needed in terms of feedback but was more interested in seeing what mattered most to each tester. Some commented on the process, some were helpful about the taste and texture of each dish, and others paid special attention to the leftovers or shopping lists.

This week was tested by a biology professor who is a working mom with two kids. All of it mattered to her, and her comments and suggestions were detailed and precise. I sat a little straighter in my chair when her feedback came in, as you would when your favourite teacher read your rough copy. Other testers were perhaps a little easier on me, but their efforts were no less valuable. Learning what "mom on the street" wants from this book has given me a wealth of understanding and I thank all of my testers. So will you!

Standards Face Lift

*Roasted Vegetables with Garlic Oil

Chicken Cacciatore

Salmon Cakes with Caper Mayo

*Baked Pork Tenderloin with Spinach and Blue Cheese
with Tomato Salad

WORK SCHEDULE

1 Clean, chop and bake vegetables for Roasted Vegetables with Garlic Oil.
2 Complete Chicken Cacciatore recipe up to simmer then start on salmon.
3 Microwave salmon for Salmon Cakes then let cool while you make Mayo and
   divide for Salmon Cakes as well as dip.
4 Continue with salmon recipe up to cornmeal step. Freeze for later in the week.
5 Start pork tenderloin recipe and store in fridge until ready to cook for tonight's
   supper. Continue with Tomato Salad. Cover and refrigerate.
6 Complete Chicken Cacciatore and freeze for later in the week.

*Serve it tonight.

Roasted Vegetables with Garlic Oil

SERVES
4+2

PREPARATION TIME
20 MINUTES

The beautiful part of this recipe is its ignorability. It cooks in about 30 minutes but can be left for up to 1 1/2 hours in the oven.

1 large globe eggplant	6 Italian plum (Roma)	Salt and pepper to taste
4 small zucchini	tomatoes	1/4 cup (50 mL) dry Italian
1 medium sweet red pepper	1 small onion	bread crumbs
	2 tbsp (30 mL) garlic oil	1 tbsp (15 mL) dried basil

- Cut eggplant into chunks about one-quarter the size of your palm. Cut zucchini in half lengthwise. Seed, core and cut red pepper in half lengthwise; cut in half again. Halve tomatoes. Slice onion into rings.
- Brush large roasting pan or 2 baking dishes with half of the garlic oil. Arrange vegetables in one layer in pan; brush with remaining garlic oil. Sprinkle with salt and pepper. Bake in 350°F (180°C) oven until tender, stirring once or twice, about 30 minutes.
- Remove to serving platter. Sprinkle with bread crumbs and basil. Cover lightly with plastic wrap and let stand for up to 2 hours. Serve at room temperature or broil for 3 minutes to reheat.

Tip

If garlic oil is hard to find, try any seasoned oil. Or make your own by squeezing 2 cloves of garlic into 1 cup (250 mL) olive oil. Use what you need here and store the rest in the fridge for up to 4 weeks. For a quick way to make garlic bread, spread with seasoned oil and broil.

Grab and Go

Roasted Vegetable Pasta: Leftover vegetables can be chopped into a midweek pasta dish. Cover with 1/4 cup (50 mL) olive oil and 2 tbsp (30 mL) balsamic vinegar; refrigerate in airtight container for up to 4 days. Boil water for whole wheat pasta. Use large microwaveable bowl to mix 1 can (19 oz/540 mL) lupini beans, drained, with 1 clove garlic, crushed. Toss in reserved veggies with liquid and microwave at high for 3 to 5 minutes. When pasta is cooked, toss with vegetables in bowl. Chopped fresh basil and grated Parmesan cheese are welcome toppings.

Chicken Cacciatore

SERVES
4+4

PREPARATION TIME
12 MINUTES

Some kids don't like things all cooked together so I often cook a few pieces of chicken thoroughly and keep them separate. I'll serve the sauce alongside as a dip.

2 lb (1 kg) boneless skinless chicken thighs
2 tsp (10 mL) canola oil
1 onion, cut into rings
1 sweet green pepper, cored, seeded and chopped
6 cloves garlic

2 cans (each 24 oz/680 mL) tomato sauce
2 tsp (10 mL) dried oregano
2 tsp (10 mL) dried basil
1 tsp (5 mL) dried rosemary
1/2 tsp (2 mL) dried thyme
1/2 tsp (2 mL) hot pepper flakes

1/4 tsp (1 mL) pepper
2 dashes Tabasco sauce
8 oz (250 g) mushrooms, sliced, optional
1/4 cup (50 mL) fresh parsley, chopped, optional

- Cut chicken into pieces one-quarter the size of your palm. Heat large deep pot then add oil. Add chicken in 2 batches; brown, letting pan reheat before adding second batch. Remove from pan and set aside.
- Add onion, green pepper and garlic; cook until onion is tender.
- Add tomato sauce, oregano, basil, rosemary and thyme to pot. Return chicken to pot; simmer over medium-low heat, uncovered, for 45 minutes, stirring occasionally.
- Add red pepper flakes, pepper and Tabasco sauce. Add mushrooms, and parsley, if desired. Refrigerate half up to 3 days in single-serving portions. Freeze remaining portions up to 4 weeks. Thaw in microwave or in saucepan. Cook, uncovered, 5 minutes or until sauce is desired consistency.

Tips

I recommend rinsing the chicken under cold tap water and drying with paper towel since the processing of chicken can leave its own residue. Be very careful to use a separate sink if you have 2 and keep other foods away until you have cleaned up well.

Chicken thighs are much juicier and higher in iron than breasts even though the fat content is higher.

This is a leaner version of spaghetti sauce that is great served over pasta. Try spelt or whole wheat pasta for an improvement, but if your kids are really picky, even spinach pasta is better than white. (Other colours are usually no improvement to the nutritional value of pasta.)

Grab and Go

This is a great dish for sending in a vacuum bottle for lunch or for eating in the car on your way to hockey practice. Add a few mini whole wheat pitas and it is a meal; no need to serve with pasta at all.

Salmon Cakes with Caper Mayo

SERVES
4+4

PREPARATION TIME
15 MINUTES

Salmon is rich in omega-3 fatty acids, but you will serve these because they taste great. The colour of these cakes alone is appetizing, and the taste is a delicate balance of sweet seafood with salty additions.

2 lb (1 kg) fresh salmon fillets	1 cup (250 mL) light mayonnaise	1/2 cup (125 mL) cornmeal
1/4 cup (50 mL) lime or lemon juice	2 tbsp (30 mL) Dijon mustard	2 tbsp (30 mL) olive oil
1 cup (250 mL) finely chopped green onion	1 tsp (5 mL) chili powder	2 tsp (10 mL) unsalted butter
1 cup (250 mL) finely chopped fresh cilantro or parsley	2 tbsp (30 mL) drained capers	1 pkg (10 oz/300 g) mixed fresh greens
	1 1/3 cups (325 mL) dry Italian seasoned bread crumbs (approx)	1 bunch fresh mint

Tips

These cakes are a good way to introduce fish to your kids. Feel free to serve on whole wheat buns with ketchup and mustard to present them like burgers if that is what it takes. Adults are satisfied with a couple of cakes and a salad.

Cornmeal makes great cornbread, but an even easier way to use it up is to make polenta. Boil 2 cups (500 mL) water and add 1/2 cup (125 mL) cornmeal; simmer and stir for 10 to 15 minutes until it becomes very gooey. Add 1 tbsp (15 mL) butter and salt and pepper to taste for a whole-grain side dish. Any leftovers can be emptied into a cake pan, covered and refrigerated overnight.You can cut squares and fry them for breakfast.

Skip the green stuff if your children turn green just thinking about it. Slip them some fresh mint as a garnish; there is folic acid in it and they will eat it.

- Break fish into pieces; place on microwaveable plate. Cover with vented plastic wrap; microwave at high for 6 to 8 minutes until opaque. Scrape flesh from skin and crumble salmon into bowl; drizzle with lime juice. Add green onion and cilantro; mix lightly with fork.

- In separate bowl, mix mayonnaise, mustard and chili powder; add half to salmon and mix with fork. Add capers to remaining mayonnaise mixture for Caper Mayo; set aside.

- Mix bread crumbs into salmon mixture until it holds together, adding more bread crumbs, 1 tbsp (15 mL) at a time, if necessary. Form into 8 cakes, approximately 3 inches (8 cm) in diameter and 3/4 inch (2 cm) thick. Roll in cornmeal to coat. Cover with plastic wrap and refrigerate for at least 30 minutes and up to 24 hours. (Cakes can be frozen, separated by plastic wrap, in airtight container.)

- In heavy skillet, heat oil and butter over medium-high heat; fry cakes until crisp and golden brown on bottom, 3 to 5 minutes. Turn carefully only once; brown other side. Cover and let warm through, 8 to 10 minutes. Serve with Caper Mayo.

- (Freeze unused cakes individually wrapped in plastic wrap then placed in resealable plastic bag for up to 2 weeks. Cook from frozen over medium to medium-low heat for 15 to 20 minutes.)

Baked Pork Tenderloin with Spinach and Blue Cheese with Tomato Salad

SERVES
4+2

This is baked in a casserole dish but its components remain separate which is the best of both worlds, an easy method producing a meal that kids will eat.

PREPARATION TIME
12 MINUTES

2 pork tenderloins, 16 oz
 (500 g) each
3 pkg (each 10 oz/300 g)
 frozen chopped spinach,
 thawed and drained
1/4 cup (50 mL) red wine
2 cloves garlic, minced

2 tbsp (30 mL) balsamic
 vinegar
2 tsp (10 mL) dried oregano
Salt and pepper to taste
6 oz (175 g) blue cheese,
 crumbled

Tomato Salad:
2 cups (500 mL) cherry
 tomatoes, cut in half
1/2 cup (125 mL) fresh basil,
 chopped
2 cloves garlic, minced
Salt and pepper to taste

- Cut each pork tenderloin into 4 equal portions on diagonal. Spread spinach in shallow casserole dish large enough to hold pork without squeezing. Nestle pork in spinach. Sprinkle with wine, garlic, vinegar, oregano, salt and pepper. Crumble blue cheese on and around pork, leaving some uncovered if blue cheese is not popular. Cover with foil and refrigerate for up to 24 hours or freeze for up to 2 weeks.

- Tomato Salad: In separate bowl, toss cherry tomatoes with basil, garlic, salt and pepper. (Salad can be covered and refrigerated for up to 24 hours.)

- Cover and roast pork in 350°F (180°C) oven for 20 to 25 minutes until meat thermometer registers 160°F (70°C) and hint of pink remains inside. Serve with Tomato Salad. (Pork can be sliced, wrapped in plastic wrap and refrigerated up to 3 days or frozen up to 3 weeks.)

Tips

Frozen chopped spinach is the bargain of the century both nutritionally and financially. It is picked at its peak, cleaned (and we know what a pain that can be!), chopped and frozen. It is the second healthiest vegetable in our food system (next to kale) and it is always less than $2.

Use cream cheese as a substitute for blue cheese for a milder dish. If this recipe is a hit, next time double the ingredients and make two casseroles. The second can be frozen, wrapped in foil from the bottom up. Thaw in the fridge about 48 hours before roasting as directed.

Grab and Go

Pork and Cabbage Stir-Fry: Use leftover slices of pork in a stir-fry. In large skillet, heat 1 tbsp (15 mL) canola oil; add one 16 oz (454 g) pkg coleslaw. Toss with 1/4 cup (50 mL) low-sodium soy sauce and 2 tbsp (30 mL) honey. Stir in 1 to 2 tbsp (15 to 30 mL) toasted sesame oil. Slice pork into thin strips; stir in to reheat. Cook some egg noodles on the side; they are faster than rice and contain some extra protein from the eggs.

Grab and Go

Spinach and Blue Cheese Lunch Wrap: Any extra spinach with blue cheese is a great lunch if wrapped in a whole wheat tortilla with a few slices of smoked turkey or prosciutto. Warm in microwave for 1 minute before serving.

Week 3 Shopping List

YOU NEED:

*Mini pitas (1 pkg)
*Whole wheat tortillas (1 pkg)
Blue cheese (6 oz/175 g)
Grated Parmesan cheese (1/4 cup/
   50 mL)
*Smoked turkey or prosciutto (12 slices)
Fresh salmon fillets (2 lb/1 kg)
Frozen chopped spinach (3 pkg,
   10 oz/300 g each)
Boneless skinless chicken thighs
   (2 lb/1 kg)
Pork tenderloins (2 lb/1 kg)
Mixed greens (1 pkg, 10 oz/300 g)
*Coleslaw mix (1 pkg, 16 oz/454 g)
Green pepper (1)
Roma or plum tomatoes (6)
Red pepper (1)
Zucchini (4 small)
Onions (2 small)
Lime or lemon juice (1/4 cup/50 mL)
Mushrooms (8 oz/250 g)
Green onions (1 bunch)
Cherry tomatoes (2 cups/500 mL)
Fresh basil (1 bunch)
Fresh cilantro (2 bunches)
Fresh mint (1 bunch)
Globe eggplant (1 large)
Garlic (11 cloves)
Fresh parsley (1/4 cup/50 mL)

CHECK YOUR PANTRY FOR:

Red wine (1/4 cup/50 mL)
Italian seasoned bread crumbs
   (1 2/3 cups/425 mL)
*Lupini beans (1 can, 19 oz/540 mL)
Tabasco sauce (2 dashes)
Dijon mustard (2 tbsp/30 mL)
*Honey (2 tbsp/30 mL)
Garlic oil (2 tbsp/30 mL)
Canola oil (2 tbsp/30 mL)
*Olive oil (2 tbsp/30 mL + *1/4 cup/
   50 mL)
Unsalted butter (2 tsp/10 mL)
Cornmeal (1/2 cup/125 mL)
Capers (2 tbsp/30 mL)
*Whole wheat pasta (1 pkg, 2 lb/900 g)
*Egg noodles (1 pkg, 13 oz/375 g)
Light mayonnaise (1 cup/250 mL)
*Toasted sesame oil (2 tbsp/30 mL)
*Low-sodium soy sauce (1/4 cup/
   50 mL)
Chili powder (1 tsp/5 mL)
Dried basil (2 tbsp/30 mL)
Hot pepper flakes (1/2 tsp/2 mL)
Dried thyme (1/2 tsp/2 mL)
Tomato sauce (2 cans, 24 oz/680 mL
   each)
Dried oregano (4 tsp/20 mL)
Dried rosemary (1 tsp/5 mL)
Balsamic vinegar (2 tbsp/30 mL
   + *2 tbsp/30 mL)

*grab and go items

Notes

WEEK 4

I am lucky enough to have some of Toronto's best and brightest dieticians refer their clients to me. This happens when a client has learned that dietary improvements need to be made but needs help with the transition. With each referral, I learn a little more about specific dietary needs. One devoted healthcare researcher and nutritional counsellor, Aileen Burford-Mason, is someone who can give you more information in five minutes than you could learn by yourself in a year. Her views are perhaps more "hard line" than mine, allowing no room for junk. I'm more "disguise and conquer." Aileen and I had a discussion about white rice that influenced this entire book.

I know that most of you are still eating white rice and I originally wrote most recipes for white rice (brown rice optional). Aileen encouraged me not to water down the message and to go the other way, using brown rice in recipes, making the white version the alternative. "If, and only if, it tastes better," I said. The result? You will find whole-grain brown rice in all of these recipes, and I encourage you to try them this way. They do taste better. Of course, nutritionally they really are better, whether you are counting carbs, vitamins and minerals or fibre. Aileen and brown rice win.

Warming Food for Chilly Days

Veggies

Chicken Soup

✳ Rice with Grated Carrots

Meat Loaf Florentine with Salsa

✳ Jamaican-ish Pork

WORK SCHEDULE

1 Clean Veggies first so your carrots and celery are ready when you make the soup.
2 Complete Chicken Soup and freeze in single-serving sizes.
3 Start rice for Rice with Grated Carrots to serve tonight with Jamaican-ish Pork.
4 Prepare meat loaf, wrap in foil and bake. Freeze.
5 Marinate Jamaican-ish Pork until you are ready to bake for tonight's supper.

✳Serve it tonight.

Veggies

SERVES
4

PREPARATION TIME
20 MINUTES

Cleaning and chopping vegetables at the start of your cooking session means less work as you are in the process. Plus, it is always handy to have veggies ready when hunger hits.

1 head celery	1 each sweet red and yellow	1 head broccoli
2 lb (1 kg) carrots	pepper	

- Set aside 2 celery stalks and 4 carrots for soup as well as rice dish. Clean, slice and refrigerate red and yellow peppers, broccoli and remaining celery and carrots in resealable plastic bags with a piece of paper towel up to 5 days.

Tips

Store veggies in a large freezer bag with one square of paper towel. Replace paper towel each time you open the bag as it absorbs the excess moisture, keeping veggies fresh longer.

Store peppers separately as they soften quicker and can hasten the spoilage of other vegetables.

Chicken Soup

SERVES
4+2

PREPARATION TIME
30 MINUTES

There's nothing more comforting than chicken soup, especially when you feel a cold coming on.

6 cups (1.5 L) chicken stock (preferably homemade or frozen)	1 1/2 lb (750 g) boneless skinless chicken breast halves or thighs	1 tsp (5 mL) poultry seasoning 1 clove garlic
1 cup (250 mL) baby carrots	1 onion, chopped	1 cup (250 mL) frozen corn
2 stalks celery	1 tsp (5 mL) garlic powder	1 cup (250 mL) frozen peas Salt and pepper to taste

- In large saucepan, bring chicken stock to boil. Meanwhile, chop carrots and celery into small dice; set aside.
- Rinse chicken and cut into dollar-size pieces. Add to stock and simmer for 5 minutes. Skim foam from top.
- Add carrots, celery, onion and garlic powder; simmer for 10 minutes.
- Add poultry seasoning and garlic. Stir in corn and peas; simmer 1 more minute. Add salt and pepper. (Refrigerate in small containers up to 3 days or freeze up to 1 month.)

Frozen real chicken stock is always best but if you use the canned type be sure to add extra water to cut the salt.

Rice with Grated Carrots

This is the simplest rice recipe that's as pretty as can be. Make it again to serve with Meat Loaf Florentine, if you like.

3 cups (750 mL) chicken
   stock or water
1 1/2 cups (375 mL) brown rice

2 carrots, grated
2 tsp (10 mL) fresh thyme
   leaves

1/2 tsp (2 mL) butter
Salt and pepper to taste

- In large saucepan, bring stock to boil. Add rice; cover and simmer for 30 to 40 minutes or until tender and no liquid remains. Stir in carrots, thyme leaves, butter, salt and pepper.

SERVES
4+2

PREPARATION TIME
5 MINUTES

This rice is bland enough for fussy kids. To add a splash of spice, add 1 tbsp (15 mL) Mexican Dressing (page 141).

Experiment with the brown rices now available, such as brown basmati, which cooks quickly. The short-grain brown sushi rice has a great stickiness that kids seem to like.

To store, transfer to casserole dish; top with more grated carrot and sprig of thyme. Sprinkle with 1 tsp (5 mL) olive oil to keep top from drying out; place plastic wrap on top. Cover and refrigerate up to 24 hours.

Grab and Go
Egg-Fried Rice: Leftover rice is perfect for Chinese stir-fried rice. Heat 1 tbsp (15 mL) canola oil in large skillet; add 1 egg and scramble; remove to large bowl. Add 2 cups (500 mL) peas to pan and cook until tender. Allow pan to reheat between additions and continue adding oil to cook one vegetable at a time. (Try frozen corn, grated carrot, green onions, etc.) Fry rice last in small batches so it does not stick. (Unfortunately, this must be done with generous amount of oil and at high heat but adding lots of vegetables will balance the downside of this method.) Toss together ingredients in a bowl like a salad and sprinkle with soy sauce.

Meat Loaf Florentine with Salsa

SERVES
4+6

Traditional meat loaf has too much fat and no fibre. This version changes that with the additions of spinach and salsa.

PREPARATION TIME
20 MINUTES

2 lb (1 kg) lean ground beef
1 cup (250 mL) seasoned
    bread crumbs
1/4 cup (50 mL) barbecue
    sauce or ketchup
2 eggs

3 tbsp (45 mL) dried onion
2 tbsp (30 mL) garlic powder
4 tsp (20 mL) dried oregano
2 tbsp (30 mL) poultry
    seasoning
Salt and pepper to taste

Topping:
2 pkg (10 oz/300 g each)
    frozen chopped spinach,
    thawed
1 cup (250 mL) grated
    Parmesan cheese
1 tbsp (15 mL) dried oregano
Salt and pepper to taste
2 cups (500 mL) salsa

Tips

If your kids don't like meat loaf, use an ice cream scoop and serve in round balls called . . . meatballs.

You could substitute ground pork, chicken or turkey in this recipe; just scale up the bread crumbs a little to make sure the loaf is not too crumbly because the water content of these substitutes is higher.

• In large bowl and using fork, mix beef, bread crumbs, barbecue sauce, eggs, onion, garlic powder, oregano, poultry seasoning, salt and pepper. Divide and firmly pat into 5 foil mini loaf pans until two-thirds full only.

• Topping: Squeeze some liquid out of spinach; place in large bowl. Mix with Parmesan cheese, oregano, salt and pepper. Divide and pat over meat mixture firmly with fork. Cover with foil.

• Place meat thermometer through foil and into centre of one of the loaves without touching edges of pan. Bake loaves on baking sheet in 425°F (220°C) oven for 1 to 1 1/2 hours or until meat thermometer registers 170°F (77°C). Let cool for 20 minutes. Refrigerate for up to 3 days or freeze for up to 6 weeks.

• To reheat, thaw in fridge overnight. (Each loaf should serve 2 or 3 adults.) Bake in 350°F (180°C) oven for 45 to 60 minutes. Invert onto platter, cut into 4 slices. Serve with salsa on the side.

Grab and Go
Second-time Sloppy Joes: Thaw one loaf. Break up or chop into small pieces and stir into a pot containing your favourite tomato sauce. Mash with a fork as it cooks and serve over whole wheat Kaiser buns.

Jamaican-ish Pork

SERVES
4+6

PREPARATION TIME
11 MINUTES

Use the largest tenderloin to serve 4 tonight. Freeze the others and expect to serve 3 with each. Serve with bean salad on mixed greens along with some whole grain bread.

2 tsp (10 mL) olive oil
6 cloves garlic, minced
3 tbsp (45 mL) chopped fresh
   thyme
4 tsp (20 mL) chili powder

1 tbsp (15 mL) allspice
1 tbsp (15 mL) pepper
1 tsp (5 mL) ground cumin
3/4 tsp (4 mL) salt

1/2 tsp (2 mL) cinnamon
1/2 tsp (2 mL) nutmeg
3 pork tenderloins, 12–16 oz
   (375–500 g) each

- In bowl, combine oil with garlic, thyme, chili powder, allspice, pepper, cumin, salt, cinnamon and nutmeg; add pork, turning to coat. Transfer to 3 large resealable plastic bags. Refrigerate 1 bag up to 24 hours; freeze remaining 2 bags for up to 3 weeks. Thaw before cooking.
- Transfer pork to roasting pan; roast in 450°F (230°C) oven for 30 to 40 minutes until meat thermometer registers 160°F (70°C). Let stand for 5 minutes before cutting.

Fresh thyme will keep for up to a month wrapped in plastic in the crisper of the fridge, but if you dry it, it will keep for up to 6 months in your cupboard. Rinse thyme and pat dry with paper towel then lay out on a baking sheet covered in foil. When you have finished baking the tenderloin, turn the oven off and place the thyme in the oven for up to 4 hours until dried. Then place the entire stems in resealable plastic bags.

Grab and Go

Jamaican Roti: Slice leftover pork into thin strips and toss with any remaining bean salad. Serve over remaining rice on a roti or other flatbread with hot sauce.

Week 4 Shopping List

YOU NEED:

*Whole wheat Kaiser buns (3)
*Whole wheat tortillas (1 pkg)
Whole grain bread (1 loaf)
*Roti (1 pkg)
*eggs (3)
Grated Parmesan cheese
    (1 cup/250 mL)
Lean ground beef (2 lb/1 kg)
Pork tenderloins (3)
Boneless skinless chicken breasts
    or thighs (1 1/2 lb/750 g)
Frozen chopped spinach
    (2 pkg, 10 oz/300 g each)
Frozen corn (1 cup/250 mL)
Frozen peas (1 cup/250 mL
    + *2 cups/500 mL)
Onion (1)
Mixed greens (1 pkg)
Garlic (7 cloves)
Red pepper (1)
Yellow pepper (1)
Carrots (2 1/4 lb/625 g)
Baby carrots (1 cup/250 mL)
Green onions (1 bunch)
Broccoli (1 head)
Celery (2 heads)
Fresh thyme (1/4 cup/50 mL)
Mini foil loaf pans (5)

CHECK YOUR PANTRY FOR:

Seasoned bread crumbs (1 cup/250 mL)
Mixed bean salad (1 jar)
Barbecue sauce or ketchup
    (1/4 cup/50 mL)
*Hot sauce (1 small bottle)
Olive oil (2 tsp/10 mL)
Canola oil (1 tbsp/15 mL)
Brown basmati rice
    (1 1/2 cups/375 mL)
Chicken stock (9 cups/2.25 L)
Poultry seasoning (7 tsp/35 mL)
Dried onion (3 tbsp/45 mL)
Dried oregano (7 tsp/35 mL)
Garlic powder (7 tsp/35 mL)
Chili powder (4 tsp/20 mL)
Allspice (1 tbsp/15 mL)
Ground cumin (1 tsp/5 mL)
Cinnamon (1/2 tsp/2 mL)
Nutmeg (1/2 tsp/2 mL)
*Tomato sauce (2 cans, 18 oz/532 mL
    each)
Butter (1/2 tsp/2 mL)
Salsa (2 cups/500 mL)
Soy sauce (1 tbsp/15 mL approx)

*grab and go items

Notes

WEEK 5

When I discovered that kale topped the list of healthy vegetables, I set out to make it palatable. I mean, let's face it, it's green, a little bitter and smells strong when cooked. One day I was drying herbs and a bunch of kale was just sitting there, on the verge of being released into compost heaven. What would I do with *it* if *it* were a batch of thyme that I pulled out of the garden just in time to build a snowman around it? I would dry it.

So I rinsed it, laid it out on a baking sheet and sprinkled on some flavourings that are well liked in this house: chili powder, garlic, salt. I stuck it into the oven and walked the dog around the block. Upon my return, the house smelled slightly spicy and like roasted vegetables. To my surprise, the greens came up crispy and tasty. When I handed my daughter a bowl of this flaky green stuff as an afterschool snack (get 'em when they're hungry!), she daintily plucked out a leaf, then more heartily chomped on the rest of the bowl. You know the joy I am talking about, the relief, the high-fiving yourself in the kitchen when they actually eat something good for them.

We have since served this Krispy Kale as an hors d'oeuvre and have also crushed and sprinkled it on pasta for some colour and flavour. When my daughter returns home to the smell of drying kale she actually cheers "Yeah, kale!" I, of course, giggle inwardly while I admonish her not to eat too much and to leave some for the others.

Ham Bone into Hearty Soup

Sunday Ham Soup with Romano Beans and Kale

✳Slow-Cooked Beer-Braised Beef

✳Red Pepper Rice

✳Steamed Broccoli

Five-Spice Chicken with Hot Slaw

WORK SCHEDULE

1 Simmer the ham bone for Sunday Ham Soup up to three hours but as little as one hour will do in a pinch.
2 Brown the beef for the Slow-Cooked Beer-Braised Beef and continue with recipe until the pot goes into the oven.
3 Microwave rice for Red Pepper Rice.
4 Prepare broccoli to serve tonight with Beer-Braised Beef but store in fridge covered in plastic until 10 minutes before supper.
5 Start Five-Spice Chicken with Hot Slaw to freezing point. Freeze for later in the week.
6 Complete Sunday Ham Soup.

✳Serve it tonight.

Sunday Ham Soup with Romano Beans and Kale

SERVES
8

PREPARATION TIME
20 MINUTES

As with many great discoveries, this was a happy accident. The smokiness of the ham highlights the kale while the beans provide a soft comfort.

10 cups (2.5 L) water	1 dried ancho chili	1 can (19 oz/540 mL) romano
1 ham bone	1/2 cup (125 mL) orzo	beans
2 cups (500 mL) vegetable	3 cups (750 mL) coarsely	1/4 tsp (1 mL) ground cloves
scraps	chopped, rinsed kale	

The ham bone and vegetable scraps used in the recipe can come from Week 2 (see Tips, pages 20 and 22).

Orzo is a rice-shaped pasta that is great as a side dish. Simply cook like pasta and toss with butter, salt, pepper and some grated Parmesan cheese.

Extras can be refrigerated up to 4 days but omit the orzo if you are going to freeze this dish, since pasta tends to get grainy and mushy as it continues to absorb liquid.

Use whatever old or wilted vegetables that you have on hand or have frozen over the week to make the stock.

- In large pot, bring water, ham bone, vegetable scraps and ancho chili to boil. Simmer for 1 to 3 hours (the longer, the more flavourful).
- Strain and return to pot, discarding ham bone, chili and vegetables. (If spicy soup is desired, scrape out and discard seeds from chili; break chili into pieces and return to pot.) Freeze at this point (see Tip), or carry on with cooking instructions to serve within 4 days.
- Bring stock to boil; add orzo and cook for 5 minutes. Add kale, beans and cloves; simmer for 5 minutes.

Grab and Go

Krispy Kale: Rinse kale well under running water and pat dry with paper towels. Tear leaves into potato chip–sized pieces; discard stems. Lay kale in single layer on one or two baking sheets. Sprinkle with chili powder, garlic powder and salt to taste. Bake at 350°F (180°C) until crisp but not browned, about 15 minutes. Turn oven off; leave kale in oven with door ajar until crisp and cool. Store in hard-sided airtight containers. Serve as a side dish or appetizer.

Slow-Cooked Beer-Braised Beef

SERVES
4

Serve with rye bread and steamed broccoli. This can be prepared on the stovetop if you don't have a slow-cooker.

PREPARATION TIME
10 MINUTES

1 tbsp (15 mL) canola oil   **1 onion, sliced**   **1 tsp (5 mL) pepper**
2 lb (1 kg) beef chuck roast   **1 tsp (5 mL) soy sauce**   **4 tsp (20 mL) dried basil**
1 bottle (340 mL) beer

- Heat large pot over high heat; add oil. Brown roast on all sides. Add beer, onion, soy sauce, pepper and basil; bring to boil. Cover and place pot in 275°F (140°C) oven for 6 to 8 hours or until meat is tender.
- To use a slow-cooker, omit oil and place beef directly into cooker. Top with remaining ingredients. Cook on high for 1 hour; reduce heat to low and cook for up to 8 hours.
- (Store sliced in fridge up to 3 days.)

Use rye bread to sop up the juices. Be sure that rye flour is the first ingredient on the list, otherwise it is glorified white bread. Rye is lower on the glycemic index so it is absorbed more slowly by your body causing a slower rise in insulin.

Grab and Go

Hot Beef au Jus: Slice meat and store with its juices. Beef is great in lunch boxes or served as a hot beef sandwich later in the week with some mustard and horseradish for the adults.

Steamed Broccoli

SERVES
4

PREPARATION TIME
5 MINUTES

Many grocery stores carry packaged broccoli florets that are a
time saver.

Even kids who don't like green
vegetables may try them raw.
Remember that kids need to see
the same food anywhere from
seven to 20 times before they will
try it. Don't give up. Just keep putting out ridiculously small portions. Try serving broccoli in an
eggcup filled with a spoonful of
melted butter. Sometimes presentation goes a long way. A baby
tree in the eggcup is worth two in
the vegetable bin.

When a steamer is beyond your energy level, the microwave does a good job, fast.

1 bunch broccoli, cut into florets	**1 tbsp (15 mL) white wine** **1 tsp (5 mL) lemon juice**	**Pinch each salt and pepper**

• Place broccoli in large microwaveable bowl; sprinkle with wine, lemon juice, salt and pepper. (Can be covered with plastic wrap and refrigerated up to 24 hours.)

• Microwave, covered, on high for 5 to 7 minutes until bright green and crisp-tender.

Red Pepper Rice

SERVES
4+2

PREPARATION TIME
3 MINUTES

This is a simple, microwaveable side dish that you will use often.

3 cups (750 mL) water **1 1/2 cups (375 mL) brown basmati rice**	**1 tsp (5 mL) salt** **1 sweet red pepper**	**1 tsp (5 mL) butter** **Pepper to taste**

• In large microwaveable bowl, combine water, rice and salt; cover with plastic wrap. Seed, core and grate red pepper into small bowl; cover with plastic wrap. Microwave rice on high for 5 minutes; fluff with fork and microwave on defrost level for 10 minutes or until tender.

• Add red pepper, butter and pepper; stir with fork, cover with plastic wrap and let sit 5 minutes before serving. (Can be refrigerated for 24 hours.)

Brown rice needs to be a staple
in your home; if you are having
trouble making the switch, brown
basmati is a good one. It has
more flavour and a less chewy
texture than regular brown rice.

Grab and Go

Chicken-Fried Rice: Heat 1 tbsp (15 mL) canola oil in large skillet. Break up some ground chicken into skillet and stir-fry until fully cooked. Pour off all liquid and remove to large bowl. Add 2 cups (500 mL) chopped celery to skillet; stir-fry until tender and add to bowl. Carry on with other veggies, reheating pan between additions (try chopped broccoli, green onions, etc.) and adding oil as needed. Fry rice last in small batches so it does not stick. Toss together ingredients in a bowl and sprinkle with soy sauce.

Five-Spice Chicken with Hot Slaw

SERVES
4

PREPARATION TIME
15 MINUTES

Grated cabbage isn't just for coleslaw anymore. It is a healthy vegetable that goes well with Asian flavours.

16 skinless chicken drumsticks	1/4 cup (50 mL) brown sugar	1 pkg (16 oz/454 g) coleslaw cabbage mix
1/2 cup (125 mL) low-sodium soy sauce	2 tbsp (30 mL) five-spice powder	

- Rinse chicken and pat dry with paper towel; divide between 2 resealable plastic bags.
- Add half the soy sauce, brown sugar and five-spice powder to each bag; seal bags and rub on all sides to blend. Refrigerate to marinate at least 1 hour or up to 48 hours. (Freeze up to 3 weeks; thaw before proceeding.)
- Spread coleslaw mix on large foil-lined baking sheet; top with chicken and marinade. Bake in 400°F (200°C) oven, uncovered, for 30 to 35 minutes, turning once, until juices run clear when chicken is pierced. Stir slaw if it starts to burn on edges.

Five-spice powder is a great Chinese staple that can usually be found in supermarkets. If you can't find it, make your own with equal parts ground aniseed, ground ginger, cinnamon and allspice. You can use five-spice powder in pumpkin pie or spice cookies; we used it to spice up a chocolate cake once and it was fabulous!

Double-duty deal: Once cooked, chicken legs can be frozen. Simply reheat in microwave for 3 to 5 minutes or serve cold. They're great for picnics.

Grab and Go

Make-Your-Own Pizza: Have on hand whole wheat pitas, shredded mozzarella cheese, smoked turkey, tomato paste, wheat germ and sliced mushrooms. Place everything on the table and let everyone build their own. Supervise the sprinkling of garlic powder, oregano and basil. Top everyone's with wheat germ to add much needed fibre as well as healthy fats. Bake in 400°F (200°C) oven for 10 to 20 minutes.

Week 5 Shopping List

YOU NEED:

*Rye bread (1 loaf)
*Whole wheat pitas (1 pkg)
*Mozzarella cheese, shredded (1 lb/
  500 g)
*Smoked turkey (8 oz/250 g)
Beef chuck roast (2 lb/1 kg)
Skinless chicken drumsticks (16)
*Ground chicken (1 lb/500 g)
*Mushrooms (6 oz/180 g)
Red pepper (1)
Kale (1 bunch + *1 bunch)
Celery (1 head)
Coleslaw cabbage mix
  (1 pkg, 16 oz/454 g)
Dried ancho chili (1)
Lemon juice (1 tsp/5 mL)
Onion (1)
Broccoli (1 bunch)

CHECK YOUR PANTRY FOR:

Brown sugar (1/4 cup/50 mL)
Beer (1 bottle)
White wine (1 tbsp/15 mL)
Romano beans (1 can, 19 oz/540 mL)
*Tomato paste (1 can, 5 1/2 oz/
  156 mL can)
Wheat germ (1 cup/250 mL
  + *2 tbsp/30 mL)
Butter (1 tsp/5 mL)
*Grainy mustard (1 tsp/5 mL)
*Horseradish (2 tsp/30 mL)
Canola oil (1 tbsp/15 mL + *1 tbsp/
  15 mL)
Brown basmati rice (1 1/2 cups/375 mL)
Ham bones or pork hock (1) – reserved
  from week 1
Soy sauce (1/2 cup + 1 tsp/130 mL
  + *1 tbsp/15 mL approx)
Orzo (1/2 cup/125 mL)
Five-spice powder (2 tbsp/30 mL)
Dried basil (4 tsp/20 mL)
Ground cloves (1/4 tsp/1 mL)
Garlic powder (2 tbsp/30 mL approx)
Dried oregano (2 tbsp/30 mL approx)
Dried basil (2 tbsp/30 mL approx)

*grab and go items

Notes

WEEK 6

No one ever cooks for me! When people find out what I do for a living they are hesitant to have me over to dinner. Listen up here and now, I will eat anything! Ask any chef what their favourite food is and they will say eggs. We are so busy cooking and thinking about the next greatest thing that we crave the ease and versatility of something simple.

That said, it is always a good idea to have a few easy crowd-pleasers in your roster. The Salmon with Spinach and Feta in Parchment is dead easy but looks as impressive as all get out. I once suggested this meal for our "mumnet" (a mother's group I belong to) weekend away. Twenty mothers in a cottage get pretty loud in the evening and lazy during the day. Sleeping in was strictly respected, so a no-fail, no-fuss recipe was a must. We prepared these packets assembly line style and baked half in the oven and half on foil on the barbecue. We devoured the contents and threw away the wrappers so no one had to do the dishes. Perfect and peaceful.

Adventurous Older Kids

Baked Mashed Potatoes and Potato Skins

Athenian Lamb and Lima Beans

✻Chicken Breasts with Spicy Rub

✻Sesame Broccoli Salad

Salmon with Spinach and Feta in Parchment

Celery Peanut Butter Logs

WORK SCHEDULE

1 Scrub and bake potatoes. Complete Mashed Potatoes and Potato Skins to freezing point. Store in fridge or freezer.
2 Start lamb recipe up to first simmer, watch and turn off until you can complete it.
3 Complete Chicken Breasts with Spicy Rub and store in fridge until you are ready to cook tonight's supper.
4 Start Sesame Broccoli Salad and leave in fridge in covered bowl until ready to bake for tonight's supper.
5 Prepare salmon and freeze in parchment packets in freezer storage bags.
6 Finish Athenian Lamb and store in fridge or freezer for future use.
7 Clean celery, cut into sticks and store in fridge, wrapped in paper towel, in resealable storage bag.

✻Serve it tonight.

Baked Mashed Potatoes and Potato Skins

SERVES
4+2

Here's an appetizer and a side dish in one.

PREPARATION TIME
15 MINUTES

6 medium baking potatoes
1/2 cup (125 mL) cream
  cheese

2 tsp (10 mL) butter or
  margarine
1 tbsp (15 mL) dried
  rosemary

1 tsp (5 mL) garlic powder
Salt to taste
3 green onions, minced
1 cup (250 mL) salsa

Potatoes have received a bad rap in recent years because they are a starchy food. However, the skin contains more potassium than a 6 ounce glass of orange juice and provides 19 percent of your vitamin B_6 as well as 10 percent of your magnesium for the day.

- Scrub potatoes; prick with fork in several places to let steam out so potatoes do not burst. Bake in 450°F (230°C) oven for 45 to 60 minutes or until tender.

- Let cool and cut in half; scoop insides into large bowl. Add cream cheese and butter; mash with potato masher. Empty into greased casserole dish; cover with plastic wrap. Refrigerate for up to 3 days or freeze for up to 3 weeks. To reheat, thaw in refrigerator if frozen. Bake in 450°F (230°C) oven, uncovered, for 30 to 45 minutes until warmed through.

- Arrange potato skins on baking sheet, sprinkle with rosemary, garlic powder and salt. Cover and refrigerate for up to 3 days or freeze on sheet until solid, place in large resealable plastic bags and store in freezer for up to 3 weeks. Reheat on baking sheet in 450°F (230°C) oven for 10 to 20 minutes. Top with green onions and serve with salsa.

Grab and Go

Fireside Supper or Porch Picnic: Kids love to simply change location once in a while, so use these potato skins as the foundation for a more casual meal. As they reheat, put out a platter of celery sticks, carrots, Cheddar cheese and rye crackers. Add a couple of pâtés (some of the veggie ones are great low-fat choices) or try smoked salmon. It may not feel like a meal to you but that is the whole point. Everyone will get fed, eat what they like, plus have a nutritious meal.

Athenian Lamb and Lima Beans

SERVES
4

PREPARATION TIME
18 MINUTES

Lamb is a great alternative to beef. Ounce for ounce, it is comparable to the nutrition and fat content of beef, but since it is still naturally grass fed and not yet in the "machine raising" process that beef is, I am choosing it over beef more often.

2 tsp (10 mL) olive oil
12 oz (375 g) lean boneless
   lamb, cubed
1 onion, chopped
4 cloves garlic, minced
1 tbsp (15 mL) dried oregano
Pinch hot pepper flakes

1 can (19 oz/540 mL) chopped
   tomatoes
1/2 tsp (2 mL) pepper
2 cups (500 mL) frozen lima
   beans, thawed
1 each sweet red and yellow
   pepper, seeded, cored and
   chopped

8 Kalamata olives, rinsed
2 tbsp (30 mL) capers, rinsed
1/4 cup (50 mL) chopped
   fresh parsley
1 lemon, sliced

- In large ovenproof pot with lid, heat half the oil over high heat; brown lamb in batches. Transfer to plate.

- Add remaining oil to pan; reduce heat to medium. Add onion, garlic, oregano and hot pepper flakes; cook, stirring, for 5 minutes or until softened.

- Return meat to pan along with any juices. Add tomatoes and pepper; bring to boil. Reduce heat, cover and simmer for 30 minutes.

- Add beans, red and yellow peppers, olives, capers and about 1/2 cup (125 mL) water to almost cover. Simmer over very low heat for 20 minutes or until lamb is tender. (To store, cool in refrigerator and store for up to 3 days or freeze for 1 month. Thaw in refrigerator overnight. Warm over medium heat.) Stir in parsley. Garnish with lemon slices.

Chicken Breasts with Spicy Rub

SERVES
4+4

PREPARATION TIME
16 MINUTES

Remove chicken skin only for those on a calorie-restricted diet and only after baking. The skin keeps the moisture in and the amount of calories and fat added is negligible if removed after baking. Be sure to rub some spice mixture under the skin if you will be removing it.

Don't be put off by the long list of ingredients. This mix is a snap and will make a big batch of rub that can be stored in the fridge up to 1 month. This is a great last-minute rub for anything on the barbecue or in the oven. Try it on extra-firm tofu and pork schnitzel.

The "spicy" here refers to flavour, not heat.

8 chicken breasts (with skin and bone), 3 lb (1.5 kg)
Spicy Rub:
1/4 cup (50 mL) ground cumin
1/4 cup (50 mL) packed brown sugar

2 tbsp (30 mL) paprika
2 tbsp (30 mL) black pepper
2 tbsp (30 mL) red wine vinegar
2 tbsp (30 mL) Dijon mustard
2 tbsp (30 mL) vegetable oil
2 tsp (10 mL) cayenne pepper

2 tsp (10 mL) curry powder
2 tsp (10 mL) salt
1 tsp (5 mL) five-spice powder
4 cloves garlic, minced
2–4 tbsp (30–60 mL) coconut milk (optional)

- Rinse chicken pieces under very cold water. Pat chicken dry with paper towel; set aside.
- Spicy Rub: In bowl, combine cumin, sugar, paprika, black pepper, vinegar, mustard, oil, cayenne pepper, curry powder, salt, five-spice powder and garlic. Add coconut milk for saucier dish. Smear all over chicken. (Refrigerate 4 in resealable plastic bag for up to 3 days and freeze remaining 4 for future use; thaw completely before baking.)
- Transfer to baking dish. Cover and bake in 325°F (160°C) oven for 35 to 45 minutes or until no longer pink inside. Uncover and bake 5 to 10 minutes to brown.

Grab and Go
Thai Finger Dinner: Slap some of the Spicy Rub on store-bought schnitzel-cut turkey or pork and sliced extra-firm tofu (about 3 cups/750 mL) and pour some apple cider or juice over top. Bake in 400°F (200°C) oven for 20 to 30 minutes. Serve with a bag of root vegetable chips.

Sesame Broccoli Salad

Here's a unique way to cook broccoli any time you have the oven on.

2 heads broccoli
1/4 cup (50 mL) sesame seeds, toasted, if possible

1/4 cup (50 mL) rice wine vinegar
1/4 cup (50 mL) low-sodium soy sauce

1 tbsp (15 mL) olive oil
1 tbsp (15 mL) toasted sesame oil
1 tsp (5 mL) grated gingerroot

- Wash broccoli. Break off florets; peel stems if desired and cut into 2-inch (5 cm) pieces. Place in bowl.
- In small bowl, combine sesame seeds, vinegar, soy sauce, olive oil, sesame oil and gingerroot; pour over broccoli. Place broccoli on large baking sheet. Bake in 325°F (160°C) oven for 30 minutes or until broccoli is soft and soaks up some of the sauce. Serve warm or at room temperature.

SERVES
8

PREPARATION TIME
20 MINUTES

Tip

A jar of grated gingerroot lasts weeks in the fridge and does not develop an off-flavour like processed garlic. Use extras in a stir-fry. Or buy just 1 inch (2.5 cm) of the fresh root at the grocery store.

Salmon with Spinach and Feta in Parchment

SERVES
4

PREPARATION TIME
20 MINUTES

Great "wow" factor for when you have company. Substitute aluminum foil for the parchment if you prefer, but the parchment does make a nicer presentation.

2 pkg (each 10 oz/300 g)
  frozen chopped spinach,
  thawed
8 oz (250 g) light feta cheese,
  crumbled

1 clove garlic, minced
1 tsp (5 mL) dried oregano
4 pieces (4 to 6 oz/125 to 175 g
  each) fresh salmon fillet

2 pieces fresh salmon fillets
  (optional extras for lunch)
1 lemon, sliced
12 chives
Salt and pepper to taste

Tips

For children who are not keen on fish, add 1 tbsp (15 mL) packed brown sugar and 1 tsp (5 mL) butter to each piece of fish. Omit spinach and add whatever vegetable they like: try grated carrots, sliced red pepper or frozen green peas.

This meal stands alone without a starch side dish but if you like try a polenta roll. These rolls are made with whole-grain cornmeal and are normally sold in the deli section or near the dried pasta. They look like a big yellow sausage wrapped in plastic. Simply cut some slices, brush with olive oil and bake on a baking sheet, uncovered, along with the salmon. The round yellow disks will complement the rectangular orange salmon.

If someone in your family hates salmon but you would like to serve this to the rest, simply substitute boneless skinless chicken breasts and proceed with the recipe. Increase baking time to 30 to 40 minutes.

- Cut 4 pieces of parchment paper about 18 inches (45 cm) long. (Cut one extra piece if you are making leftovers for lunch.) Set aside.

- Squeeze as much water as possible from spinach; break up into bowl. Crumble feta into spinach; add garlic and oregano. Divide into 4 equal mounds; place each in centre of parchment paper. Place piece of salmon on top of spinach. Top with slice of lemon and 3 chives. Sprinkle with salt and pepper.

- Lift sides of parchment and fold accordion-style, leaving a couple of inches of space for heat to circulate; crimp edges and place on baking sheet. (Freeze in resealable plastic bags for up to 2 weeks.) Bake on baking sheet in 400°F (200°C) oven 20 to 30 minutes from frozen, or 15 to 18 minutes if fresh, or until paper turns brown and puffy and fish flakes easily when tested with fork.

Grab and Go

Honey Mustard Salmon Sandwich: Mash cooked salmon with 1 tbsp (15 mL) honey mustard and 1 tbsp (15 mL) capers and place on a whole wheat hamburger bun. Wrap and refrigerate for up to 48 hours.

Celery Peanut Butter Logs

SERVES
4

PREPARATION TIME
2 MINUTES

Make sure these ingredients are on the table any time you think your kids will turn up their noses (like at the lamb stew), and they will know they have an option to make themselves an alternative.

1/2 head celery   **1/2 cup (125 mL) peanut butter**

• Clean celery stalks and let kids scoop their own peanut butter to fill the hollow.

Tip

Try switching to almond butter once in a while. It has half of the fat, is never hydrogenated and has twice the calcium of peanut butter.

Week 6 Shopping List

YOU NEED:

*Whole wheat hamburger buns (2)
*Cheddar cheese (1lb/500 g)
Cream cheese (1/2 cup/125 mL)
Light feta cheese (8 oz/250 g)
*Pâté (2 types)
Salmon fillet, 4 pieces + *2 pieces
   (4 to 6 oz/125 to 175 g each)
Boneless lamb, cubed (12 oz/375 g)
*Pork schnitzel (1lb/500 g)
Chicken breasts, bone in, 8 (3 lb/1.5 kg)
*Extra-firm tofu (12 oz/350 g)
*Carrots (2 lb/1 kg)
Green onions (3)
Red and yellow peppers (1 each)
Onion (1)
Lemons (2)
Parsley (1 bunch)
Chives (1 bunch)
Celery (1 head)
Garlic (9 cloves)
Baking potatoes (6 medium)
Gingerroot (1 tsp/5 mL grated)
Broccoli (2 heads)
Frozen chopped spinach
   (2 pkg, 10 oz/300 g each)
Frozen lima beans (2 cups/500 mL)

CHECK YOUR PANTRY FOR:

Brown sugar (1/4 cup/50 mL)
Parchment paper (1 pkg)
Canned chopped tomatoes
   (1 can, 19 oz/540 mL)
Kalamata olives (8)
Capers (2 tbsp/30 mL + *1 tbsp/15 mL)
Dijon mustard (2 tbsp/30 mL)
Honey mustard (1 tbsp/15 mL)
Toasted sesame oil (1 tbsp/15 mL)
Vegetable oil (2 tbsp/30 mL)
Olive oil (2 tbsp/30 mL)
*Whole grain rye crackers (1 pkg)
Rice crackers, any kind (1 pkg)
*Root vegetable chips (1 pkg)
Butter (2 tsp/10 mL)
*Apple cider or juice (2 cups/500 mL)
Salsa (1 cup/250 mL)
Sesame seeds (1/4 cup/50 mL)
Low-sodium soy sauce (1/4 cup/50 mL)
Coconut milk (2 tbsp/30 mL)
Peanut butter (1 cup/250 mL)
Curry powder (2 tsp/10 mL)
Cayenne (2 tsp/10 mL)
Five-spice powder (1 tsp/5 mL)
Garlic powder (1 tsp/5 mL)
Ground cumin (1/4 cup/50 mL)
Hot pepper flakes (1/2 tsp/2 mL)
Paprika (2 tbsp/30 mL)
Dried oregano (4 tsp/20 mL)
Dried rosemary (1 tbsp/15 mL)
Rice wine vinegar (1/4 cup/50 mL)
Red wine vinegar (2 tbsp/30 mL)

*grab and go items

Notes

WEEK 7

Part of my work involves teaching kids to cook (and taste). It's incredibly rewarding. They come with few preconceptions of how food should taste. I've found that once kids have invested effort in making the dish, they will be very interested in at least trying it when it's served. We encourage kids to try everything during class. We try to use the phrase "It's not my favourite" instead of "Ewwww," and we all get along just fine!

The squishy texture of the raw sausage in the Quick Italian Sausage and Kidney Bean Soup for this week put off a number of kids—until they smelled it cooking. The kidney beans were often left in the bowl but a few snuck in hungry mouths. The peppers became fun when one kid found a baby pepper inside her big one; pepper pearl diving became a sport that day.

The first time we make anything in class, it's all about exposure, not about how much gets eaten. Sausages become demystified, beans become not so bad and peppers become downright fun. Next time ingredients are more familiar and therefore more likely to be eaten. We make this soup in our cooking class often because the kids love it and it is fun. Only I know how much lycopene is in the tomato sauce, how much fibre is in the beans and that the antioxidants in the peppers will be lifelong friends.

As usual, these recipes are mostly for four servings. Just scale up to accommodate houseguests.

Houseguests!

*Asparagus in Its Own Juices

*Barley Risotto

Quick Italian Sausage and Kidney Bean Soup

Crustless Broccoli and Cheese Quiches

*Beef Tenderloin Steaks with Peppercorn Rub

WORK SCHEDULE

1 Rinse asparagus and set aside until ready to cook steaks.
2 Cook barley for Barley Risotto and store in fridge for tonight.
3 Start Quick Italian Sausage and Kidney Bean Soup up to the simmer stage. Watch and turn off after 30 minutes until you can complete it.
4 Bake Crustless Broccoli and Cheese Quiches while soup and risotto simmer. Refrigerate or freeze.
5 Prepare Peppercorn Rub and rub beef tenderloin. Wrap well in plastic wrap; store in fridge until you are ready to cook tonight's supper.
6 Complete Quick Italian Sausage and Kidney Bean Soup.

*Serve it tonight.

Asparagus in Its Own Juices

SERVES
4

PREPARATION TIME
4 MINUTES

Prepare just before reheating quiche or cooking steaks. This does not store well uncooked once the stems are cut and the lemon is added.

1 1/2 lb (750 g) fresh asparagus (the thinner the better)	1 tbsp (15 mL) water 1/2 tsp (2 mL) salt Pepper to taste	2 tbsp (30 mL) unsalted butter Half lemon

Tip

Unsalted butter tends to be a fresher product as the salt can mask the less fresh flavour. Salt in butter also causes it to hold more water, which can affect your baking.

- Cut or break off tough bottom end of asparagus and discard. (Or freeze scraps for soup.) Rinse well under cold water, wrap in a clean tea towel and store in fridge. Place asparagus on microwavable serving dish large enough to hold them slightly overlapping in sunburst pattern, tips facing in.
- Sprinkle with water, salt and pepper; dot with butter. Squeeze lemon over top. Cover with vented plastic wrap. Microwave on high for 5 minutes until bright green. (Leftovers can be covered and refrigerated up to 3 days.)

Barley Risotto

SERVES
4

PREPARATION TIME
5 MINUTES

This risotto is creamy and cheesy like the real thing but uses a healthier grain.

1 cup (250 mL) pot barley	3 cups (750 mL) chicken stock (homemade or frozen)	1/4 cup (50 mL) grated Parmesan cheese Salt and pepper to taste

Tip

Barley is healthier than rice or potatoes. Once your kids taste its chewy nuttiness, they will be more open to other more exotic grains. Try this recipe a couple of times before giving up. They may shun it at first but adding a little butter makes it taste like "baby popcorn."

- In saucepan, simmer barley in chicken stock until tender, adding water if necessary, about 50 minutes. Drain any liquid. Transfer to microwaveable dish; cool, cover and refrigerate for up to 48 hours. To serve, microwave at high for 4 to 8 minutes until hot. Stir in Parmesan cheese, salt and pepper.

Grab and Go

Barley Salad: Pour some olive oil and red wine vinegar over leftovers and add any extra asparagus. Toss in some shredded Cheddar, salt and pepper and it is a great lunch salad.

Quick Italian Sausage and Kidney Bean Soup

Recipes like these which can simmer for up to two hours make the process of cooking many things at once possible. Try to find good beef stock in the freezer section of the grocery store. It is nutritionally superior to canned, and far less salty.

4 oz (125 g) Italian sausage
1 large onion, finely chopped
2 cloves garlic, minced
2 sweet green peppers,
   seeded and chopped

2 tsp (10 mL) Italian herb
   seasoning
2 cans (19 oz/540 mL each)
   tomatoes, chopped
2 cans (19 oz/540 mL each)
   tomato sauce

2 cups (500 mL) beef stock
1 cup (250 mL) dry red wine
2 cans (19 oz/540 mL each)
   red kidney beans

- Remove casings and crumble sausage into 12- to 16-cup (3 to 4 L) saucepan. Cook over medium-high heat, stirring, until browned lightly. Add onion; cook until beginning to brown. Empty onto paper towel to drain off most of the drippings.
- Add garlic, green peppers, herb seasoning, tomatoes and their liquid, tomato sauce, beef stock and wine. Return sausage mixture to pan and bring to boil; cover, reduce heat and simmer 30 minutes. Stir in kidney beans and their liquid (which will thicken consistency of soup). If you like thinner soup, drain and rinse beans before adding.

SERVES
8

PREPARATION TIME
15 MINUTES

Tips

Aromatic with anise and other herbs, a small amount of Italian sausage gives body to this easy, chili-like soup, which is perfect to serve with crusty French bread.

If you can't find Italian seasoning, make your own by mixing dried basil, thyme, oregano and rosemary in amounts that you like. If you love basil, go heavy on that until you add up to two teaspoons (10 mL) total.

Grab and Go 1

This is a great freezer recipe. Simply scale it up and freeze what you don't serve. Freeze for up to 6 weeks in single-serving sizes to make reheating in the microwave fast and convenient.

Grab and Go 2

Sausage and Sauerkraut on a Bun: While you have the package of sausage out you may as well bake extras so they are ready for a quickie meal. Place all extra sausages on baking sheet lined with foil. Bake in 400°F (200°C) oven for 15 to 25 minutes, depending upon the thickness of the sausage. Be sure they are firm and no longer pink. You may want to broil for 2 minutes at the end to give them that barbecued look. Drain and pat with paper towel before you store in a resealable plastic bag in the fridge for 3 days or freezer for 3 weeks. They just need a quick zap in the microwave to heat. Drain a can of sauerkraut in a colander and run under cold water to remove some of the salt. The cabbage is a great, healthy vegetable, but the salt content detracts from its healthfulness. A bun, some mustard and your car keys, and soccer night never looked so simple.

Crustless Broccoli and Cheese Quiches

SERVES
6

PREPARATION TIME
10 MINUTES

I've said it before: For kids who shun green, omit the broccoli and start with fresh mint. Even one mint leaf has similar nutritional value and breaks down the myth that green stuff tastes bad! Let them pick a leaf or two and leave it at that for a week or two. Step it up to fresh basil when they seem ready. In no time, they will try fresh baby spinach and then there is no stopping the great green giant!

Serve with asparagus spears or a green salad.

2 tsp (10 mL) butter or butter-flavoured cooking spray
1 cup (250 mL) cream cheese
1 cup (250 mL) frozen broccoli

1 cup (250 mL) shredded Cheddar cheese
1/4 cup (50 mL) milk
8 extra-large eggs
1 tsp (5 mL) dried oregano

1/4 cup (50 mL) dry bread crumbs (optional)
4 sheets phyllo pastry (optional)

• Butter or spray 6 mini deep foil pie plates with cooking spray. Spread cream cheese evenly in bottoms of pans; set aside. Warm broccoli in microwave; press between paper towels until as dry as possible. Arrange over cheese.

• In large bowl, mix Cheddar cheese, milk, eggs and oregano with fork briskly. Pour over broccoli.

• If desired, sprinkle pies with bread crumbs. Lay one corner of one phyllo sheet on top of each pie and spray with cooking spray or brush with butter. Fold in half and spray again. Fold into quarters and spray again. Scrunch up edges to fit dish.

• Bake in 425°F (220°C) oven for 30 minutes until just firm. (Let cool and freeze for 4 hours. Cover with foil and refrigerate up to 48 hours or freeze up to 3 weeks. To reheat, uncover and place in cold oven then turn oven on to 350°F/180°C and bake for 30 to 40 minutes just to warm through. The gentle warming prevents rubbery eggs.)

Beef Tenderloin Steaks with Peppercorn Rub

Serve with Barley Risotto and Asparagus in Its Own Juices, if desired.

2 tsp (10 mL) pepper
2 tsp (10 mL) ground ginger
1 tsp (5 mL) ground
   cardamom
2 cloves garlic, minced

1/4 cup (50 mL) low-sodium
   soy sauce
4 beef tenderloin grilling
   steaks, 4 to 6 oz (125 to
   175 g) each

2 navel oranges
1 pkg (8 oz/227 g) mixed
   greens

SERVES
4

PREPARATION TIME
10 MINUTES

- In small bowl, combine pepper, ginger, cardamom and garlic; mix in soy sauce. Rub all over steaks. (Leave children's portions plain if desired.)
- Place steaks in roasting pan. Place plastic wrap directly on surface of meat. Let sit in refrigerator up to 8 hours. (Freeze for up to 3 weeks; thaw in refrigerator for 24 hours.) Slice oranges into wedges; store in covered bowl until ready for use.
- Roast, uncovered, in 425°F (220°C) oven for 10 to 15 minutes or until meat thermometer registers 140°F (60°C) for rare or 160°F (71°C) for medium.
- Arrange mixed greens on platter; top with steaks. Surround with orange wedges.

Bags of whole leaf salad are better than cut leaf salad, but they do go bad quickly once you open the bag. Don't be tempted to buy the lettuce from the open bins at the grocery store since the factory packaging is more hygienic. (You never know whose hands have been in those bins.) To keep the bags fresher longer, roll leaves in a paper towel.

While a little more expensive, tenderloin steaks are uniformly tender and not at all gristly. It is often the veiny texture of some cuts that turn kids off. You may omit the rub for the kids but a little soy sauce will make for good colour and flavour.

Grab and Go

Penne Straws and Peas: Most kids like tomato sauce, so we are always looking for ways to get other good nutrition into it. Here is a quick weeknight meal that requires no cooking, is low fat, meatless and contains soy which is good for all of us and the planet. Empty one can (24 oz/680 mL) tomato sauce into a pot while you boil water for pasta in another. Add 6 oz (170 g) Veggie Ground Round to the tomato sauce and warm through. Warm a big handful of frozen peas (1/2 cup/125 mL) in the pasta water for the final 2 minutes. When water boils add 2 to 4 cups (500 mL to 1 L) of whole wheat penne and cook until almost soft. Drain pasta and toss with sauce; top with Parmesan. Or, if you have any fun left in you, serve the pasta and peas (tossed with a little olive oil so it doesn't stick) with the sauce separate. Let your kids use the penne as straws to suck up the sauce. Watch little ones so they don't suck too hard and get a pea caught in the throat in their new-found zeal for peas. It's all in the presentation. Relax and laugh with a little red wine. Both are good for you.

Week 7 Shopping List

YOU NEED:

*Sandwich buns (4)
Eggs (8 extra-large)
Grated Parmesan cheese (1/4 cup/
    50 mL)
Cream cheese (1 cup/250 mL)
*Shredded Cheddar cheese (1 cup/
    250 mL + 2 tbsp/30 mL approx)
Milk (1/4 cup/50 mL)
Phyllo pastry (4 sheets)
Frozen broccoli (1 cup/250 mL)
*Frozen peas (1/2 cup/125 mL)
Pot barley (1 cup/250 mL)
Italian sausage (4 oz/125 g)
Beef tenderloin grilling steaks, 4
    (4 to 6 oz/125 to 175 g each)
*Veggie Ground Round (6 oz/170 g)
Onion (1)
Mixed greens (1 pkg)
Asparagus (1 1/2 lb/750 g)
Lemon (half)
Garlic (4 cloves)
Green peppers (2)
Navel oranges (2)
Mini foil pie pans (6)

CHECK YOUR PANTRY FOR:

Dry bread crumbs (1/4 cup/50 mL)
Chicken stock (3 cups/1.5 L)
Beef stock (2 cups/500 mL)
Dry red wine (1 cup/250 mL)
Bread crumbs (1/4 cup/50 mL)
Red kidney beans (2 cans, 19 oz/
    540 mL each)
Canned tomatoes (2 cans, 19 oz/
    540 mL each)
Tomato sauce (2 cans, 19 oz/540 mL
    each + *1 can, 24 oz/680 mL)
*Sauerkraut (1 can, 19 oz/540 mL)
Low-sodium soy sauce (1/4 cup/50 mL)
Olive oil (2 tbsp/30 mL approx)
Red wine vinegar (1 tbsp/15 mL approx)
Unsalted butter (2 tbsp/30 mL)
Butter (2 tbsp/30 mL)
*Whole wheat penne (1 pkg, 1 lb/450 g)
Dried oregano (1 tsp/5 mL)
Ground ginger (2 tsp/10 mL)
Italian herb seasoning (2 tsp/10 mL)
Ground cardamom (1 tsp/5 mL)

*grab and go items

Notes

WEEK 8

I grew up with a French-Canadian mother who would often take my sisters and me back to her childhood home, the small town of Buckingham, Quebec. It was always a place of happiness, cousins I could barely understand and food. Ma Tante and Mon Oncle were like grand-parents to me and Grandmère always smelled of home in the form of burnt toast. Here we used to sit down to a huge meal in the middle of the day when the men would come home from the factory for lunch.

My entire morning was spent playing in the wide open field out back with the smells of roasting meats and, my favourite, chicken stew and dumplings wafting out through the window. We would sit down at a table stacked with every kind of comfort food you could imagine for 12 to 18 people. I learned to love potatoes in all their forms and many vegetables free for the taking. The variety at each meal was endless and colourful. There was never any comment about what we ate or did not eat, or how much of it was good for you. It was real, well-prepared food, and you would have to be crazy to turn your nose up at anything. It was also here that I learned to say yes to sugar pie and hide it in my room until I could make space for it in my full belly.

Gone are those easy, idyllic days in my fast-paced life but I sure do close my eyes and imagine them every single time I eat Parsnip Purée Chicken Stew. It has all of the taste of tante Louise's but none of the sins that you would expect from a French-Canadian kitchen.

Classic Comfort Food

Parsnip Purée Chicken Stew

Tuna Sailboats for Kids

✳Roast Beef with Rosemary and Garlic Veggies

✳Steamed Dilly Carrots

WORK SCHEDULE

1 Cook Parsnip Purée Chicken Stew to simmer stage.
2 While chicken is simmering, prepare Tuna Sailboats and store in fridge or freezer.
3 Complete Parsnip Purée Chicken Stew and freeze.
4 Complete roast beef recipe up to and including refrigeration step until you are ready to cook tonight's dinner.
5 Steamed Dilly Carrots can be prepared and refrigerated until you are ready to cook any night's supper.

✳Serve it tonight.

Parsnip Purée Chicken Stew

SERVES
4+2

PREPARATION TIME
20 MINUTES

Most stews use flour to thicken but we use parsnips here for three reasons: to avoid the white flour starch, to add vitamins and fibre and, since it is hidden, it is impossible to pick the parsnips out!

2 lb (1 kg) boneless skinless
  chicken thighs
2 tsp (10 mL) canola oil
1 medium onion, chopped
1 tbsp (15 mL) butter
4 medium parsnips, peeled
  and cut into long chunks

2 stalks celery, chopped
1 tsp (5 mL) dried sage
1 tsp (5 mL) poultry seasoning
2 cups (500 mL) chicken
  stock
2 cups (500 mL) baby carrots,
  cut into thirds

2 cups (500 mL) frozen peas
4 small whole wheat or
  pumpernickel buns

- Rinse chicken and pat dry with paper towel; cut into 2-inch (5 cm) pieces.
- In large pot, heat oil. Stir in onion and cook on medium-high for 4 minutes. Add butter; brown chicken, in batches and without crowding. Remove from pan and set aside.
- Add parsnip, celery, sage and poultry seasoning to pot; stir for 30 seconds. Add stock and up to 2 cups (500 mL) water just to cover. Bring to boil; reduce heat to medium-low. Simmer for 12 to 15 minutes to soften parsnips. Using hand blender, purée into thicker saucelike consistency.
- Add carrots and chicken; simmer 20 to 30 minutes until juices run clear when chicken is pierced. Add peas and warm through, 1 to 3 minutes. (Freeze up to 1 month. Thaw in refrigerator overnight. Microwave at high 15 to 30 minutes depending on serving size.)
- To serve, scoop out centre of each bun; spoon stew into buns for a fun presentation.

Tuna Sailboats for Kids

A meal strictly for kids, these are meant to be eaten with little hands, played with and enjoyed.

2 cans (7 oz/200 g each) tuna, drained
2 medium carrots, grated
2 eggs

2 cups (500 mL) dry whole wheat bread crumbs
1/4 cup (50 mL) light mayonnaise

1 tbsp (15 mL) vegetable oil
2 stalks celery
2 to 4 slices whole wheat tortillas

- In large bowl, mix tuna, carrots, eggs, bread crumbs and mayonnaise until combined. Form into 8 egg-shaped patties with dip in middle to make a fat "canoe." In nonstick skillet, heat oil; fry patties on both sides until golden. (Let cool; wrap separately and refrigerate for up to 2 days. Microwave on defrost for 2 to 5 minutes to warm through.)

- To serve, slice celery into thin sticks and tortillas into triangles. Cut slit into top of tortilla triangle so celery can be threaded through. Let kids use the patty as a boat, add a celery mast and tortilla sail at the table.

SERVES
4+4

PREPARATION TIME
10 MINUTES

Tip

These are a poor man's crabcake that adults will eat. The tuna is familiar so many kids will at least try it. The omega-3 fatty acids in fish and eggs is essential for kids' growing brains.

Roast Beef with Rosemary and Garlic Veggies

SERVES
4+4

PREPARATION TIME
10 MINUTES

Freeze remaining beef stock in ice cube trays. These are better than bouillon cubes and just as convenient to add to any sauce, soup or even cooked rice. (An amazing treat for the family dog on a warm day!)

Every family loves roast beef night and together with roasted vegetables it's a complete meal. Cutting the roast in half cuts down cooking time and ensures leftovers.

8 cloves garlic	2 tbsp (30 mL) olive oil	3 lb (1.5 kg) sirloin tip oven
2 tbsp (30 mL) steak sauce	4 medium red new potatoes	roast, cut in half crosswise
1 tbsp (15 mL) Dijon mustard	1 cup (250 mL) baby carrots	1/2 cup (125 mL) beef stock
1 sprig fresh rosemary	1 medium sweet red pepper,	1 cup (250 mL) red wine
(or 1 tsp/5 mL dried)	seeded, cored and quartered	

- Using garlic press, smash garlic. Add to large shallow broiling pan. Mix in steak sauce, mustard, rosemary and oil.
- Cut potatoes into quarters. Roll potatoes, carrots and red peppers in oil mixture to coat. Spread vegetables out in pan, leaving space in centre for the 2 pieces of meat.
- Smear meat with any of the mustard mixture on bottom of pan. Pour in beef stock. (Cover and refrigerate up to 8 hours.)
- Place roasting pan in cold oven. Turn oven to 350°F (180°C); roast for 1 hour or until an instant-read thermometer reads 130°F to 135°F (54°C to 57°C) for medium-rare to medium.
- Transfer roast to cutting board; let stand for 5 minutes before carving.
- Meanwhile, broil vegetables for 2 to 4 minutes until crispy, watching closely. Place vegetables on platter. Pour red wine into pan; stir and scrape up brown bits. Serve with roast.

Grab and Go

Beef and Pasta Toss: Leftovers are great the next day for sandwiches, but if you want to create a new dish, make this pasta salad. Cook 4 cups (1 L) whole wheat penne; drain. Toss leftover meat with a 16 oz (454 g) jar of mild salsa, a small jar of marinated mushrooms and a grated carrot. Toss pasta and meat together in a large bowl and top with Parmesan cheese just before serving. A side salad completes the meal.

Steamed Dilly Carrots

SERVES
4+4

PREPARATION TIME
2 MINUTES

Two minutes prep time gives you the fastest side dish around, and kids love these sweet carrots.

2 lb (1 kg) baby carrots   **1 tbsp (15 mL) liquid honey**   **Pinch each salt and pepper**
3 tbsp (45 mL) water   **1 tsp (5 mL) dillweed**

• Into large microwaveable bowl, toss together carrots, water, honey, dillweed, salt and pepper. Cover with plastic wrap. Microwave on high for 8 to 15 minutes until crisp-tender.

Grab and Go 1
Puréed Carrot Soup: Warm leftover cooked veggies in a pot with equal amount of chicken or beef stock. Purée with handheld blender and thin as desired. Depending on the stock, you may need to add salt and pepper. Serve this with whole wheat bagels, cream cheese and smoked salmon. A side platter with raw snow peas with Mexican Dressing (page 141) will set off these colours and flavours.

Grab and Go 2
Grilled Cheese Options: Getting kids to make their own meals as early as possible is a huge bonus not only for the chief cook but also for the little one's self-esteem. Sandwich presses are a great way to get kids started. Simply lay out some butter, bread, sliced Cheddar, sliced Swiss, ham, smoked turkey and some ketchup. Let the kids build their own sandwich and place it in the grilling machine. A little help with those under 12 is a good idea since these things can get hot. Serve with the leftover steamed Dilly Carrots and ketchup. Once kids get the hang of it, they can experiment with dessert sandwich grills. Try apple pie filling and Brie, peanut butter and jam, pumpkin pie filling.

Week 8 Shopping List

YOU NEED:

*Whole wheat bagels (4)
Whole wheat or pumpernickel buns (4)
Whole wheat tortillas (6)
Eggs (2)
*Grated Parmesan cheese
   (1 cup/250 mL)
*Cream cheese (8 oz/250 g pkg)
Chicken thighs, boneless, skinless
   (2 lb/1 kg)
Sirloin tip oven roast (3 lb/1.5 kg)
*Smoked salmon (4 oz/125 g)
*Sliced Cheddar cheese (4 oz/125 g)
*Sliced Swiss cheese (4 oz/125 g)
*Sliced ham (4 oz/125 g)
*Smoked turkey (4 oz/125 g)
Onion (1)
*Mixed greens (1 pkg)
Parsnips (4)
Red new potatoes (4)
Carrots (2)
Baby carrots (3 lb/1.5 kg)
*Snow peas (4 cups/1 L)
Celery (4 stalks)
Red pepper (1)
Garlic (8 cloves)
Frozen peas (1 pkg, 1 lb/450 g)
Fresh rosemary (1 sprig)

CHECK YOUR PANTRY FOR:

Butter (1 tbsp/15 mL)
Red wine (1 cup/250 mL)
Dry bread crumbs (2 cups/500 mL)
Canned tuna (2 cans, 7 oz/200 g each)
Dijon mustard (1 tbsp/15 mL)
Steak sauce (2 tbsp/30 mL)
Olive oil (2 tbsp/30 mL)
Vegetable oil (1 tbsp/15 mL)
Canola oil (2 tsp/10 mL)
*Chicken stock, frozen (8 cups/2 L)
Beef stock (1/2 cup/125 mL)
*Whole wheat penne (1 pkg, 1 lb/450 g)
Light mayonnaise (1/4 cup/50 mL)
*Marinated mushrooms (1 small jar)
*Mild salsa (1 jar, 16 oz/454 g)
Honey (1 tbsp/15 mL)
Poultry seasoning (1 tsp/5 mL)
Dried sage (1 tsp/5 mL)
Dried dillweed (1 tsp/5 mL)

*grab and go items

Notes

WEEK 9

Once, when I had five vegetarian house-guests, I abandoned them all to go out to a party at my publishers. My guests dined on what I had left behind.

The people I met at the party that night were all impressed that I could calmly talk about the future of this book while I had a hungry houseful, but I have always been most comfortable being well ahead of schedule. As my husband has finally learned, 6 or 6:30 means 5:59 to me. Being prepared is more than just the Girl Guide's law, it is the mother's credo. When the foundations of a meal are made, then anyone can warm it up and put it on the table. Guilt disappears as the ice melts off the frozen Molasses Lentil Soup. Peace sets in when Tofu Caesar Salad needs only a bag to be opened and a toss to its leaves. Harmony happens when your guests ask for the recipe because their kids prompted them to do so. Business (studies, groceries, laundry, PTA . . .) is well under way when our lives are nourished with good food and great friends—who don't mind feeding themselves once in a while.

Scale up recipes to serve all your houseguests.

Vegetarian Visitors

Molasses Lentil Soup

Easy Minestrone

*Poppy Seed Noodles

Tofu Caesar Salad

*Lemony Baked Shrimp

*Asian Sprout and Red Pepper Salad

WORK SCHEDULE

1 The Molasses Lentil Soup and Easy Minestrone can be cooked at the same time in two separate pots, which saves steps. Chop and cook two onions together and then divide into two large pots, then continue on with the Molasses Lentil Soup recipe.

2 When you get to the stage of simmering lentils, start on Easy Minestrone. Complete both soups and store in freezer.

3 Complete Poppy Seed Noodles and store in fridge, covered.

4 Mix Tofu Caesar Salad dressing and store in fridge up to one week. Prepare and store greens.

5 Assemble Lemony Baked Shrimp, cover and store in fridge up to 6 hours until you are ready to bake for tonight's supper.

6 Toss Asian Sprout and Red Pepper Salad together and refrigerate, covered, until suppertime.

*Serve it tonight.

Molasses Lentil Soup

SERVES
8

PREPARATION TIME
18 MINUTES

The sweetness of this soup has converted many a lentil hater.

2 tsp (10 mL) canola oil	8 cups (2 L) chicken stock	1/4 cup (50 mL) lemon juice
1 onion, chopped	or water	(optional)
2 cups (500 mL) red lentils	1 cup (250 mL) frozen corn	3 tbsp (45 mL) molasses
2 red potatoes, diced	1 tbsp (15 mL) dried oregano	Salt and pepper to taste
2 carrots, diced	2 cups (500 mL) tomato juice	
	or V-8 Juice	

Using red lentils makes for pretty colour but also a fast-cooking, smooth soup. Letting your kids add a little extra molasses at the table is a good way to start them off on this one. Remember that molasses is a source of iron, not just sugar.

If you are making both soups, cook 2 onions here and remove half of the onions to second very large pot and set aside for Easy Minestrone (page 79).

- In very large pot, heat oil. Add onion; cook for about 4 minutes to soften.
- Stir red lentils, potatoes and carrots into onions. Add chicken stock and bring to boil. Reduce heat and simmer 15 minutes. Add corn, oregano, tomato juice, lemon juice if desired and molasses. Bring to simmer; cover and simmer 5 minutes. Add salt and pepper. (Refrigerate up to 4 days or freeze up to 6 weeks.)

Easy Minestrone

SERVES
8

Minus the beef and pasta, this recipe is a healthy, low-calorie choice.

PREPARATION TIME
20 MINUTES

1 tbsp (15 mL) olive oil
1 cooked chopped onion
(from Molasses Lentil
Soup, page 78) or 1 onion,
chopped
2 carrots, chopped
2 stalks celery, chopped

Half each sweet red and
green pepper, seeded,
cored and chopped
2 cloves garlic, minced
2 1/2 to 3 cups (625 to
750 mL) vegetable stock
or chicken stock
3 cups (750 mL) canned
chopped stewed tomatoes

1 leek (white and light green
part only), chopped into
rings
1 can (19 oz/540 mL) mixed
beans, drained and rinsed
1 cup (250 mL) frozen peas
3 tbsp (45 mL) bottled pesto
sauce

Stir extra pesto mixed with yogurt
into soup to enrich it just before
serving if desired.

• In large stockpot, heat oil and cooked onion over medium heat (or, heat oil; add chopped

onion and cook until softened, about 4 minutes). Add carrots, celery and red and green pep-

pers, stirring after each addition. Add garlic, stock and tomatoes; bring to boil over high heat.

Reduce heat, cover and simmer for 20 minutes or just until vegetables are tender.

• Add leek and beans; simmer for 2 minutes. Stir in frozen peas and pesto. (Refrigerate up to

5 days or freeze up to 1 month.)

Poppy Seed Noodles

SERVES
4

PREPARATION TIME
2 MINUTES

Using egg noodles boosts the protein.

| 2 cups (500 mL) egg noodles | 1 tbsp (15 mL) poppy seeds | 1 tbsp (15 mL) toasted sesame oil |

• In large pot of boiling salted water, cook noodles until just-tender; drain. Add poppy seeds and oil; toss to coat. (Refrigerate up to 2 days; serve cold or reheat in microwave for 2 minutes.)

Tip

Poppy seeds should be frozen so that they will not go rancid. Add them to any muffin or bread recipe or try making a poppy seed coffee cake as a special treat.

Grab and Go

Protein Poppy Seed Noodles: For vegetarian visitors, serve these noodles tossed with 2 cups (500 mL) mashed silken tofu to make a complete protein. They can have the Asian Sprout and Red Pepper Salad (page 83) while the rest eat their shrimp.

Tofu Caesar Salad

SERVES
4+6

PREPARATION TIME
3 MINUTES

Caesar salad is a favourite for many kids. They tend to like its creamy texure and salty nature, but we could all do without the fat-laden mayonnaise that most bottled or home recipes use. We have tried this tofu version on many Caesar-loving adults and kids and they can't taste the difference—but their bodies notice! Be sure to use the anchovy; it adds calcium and good oils. Fresh lemon juice and excellent olive oil will make a difference.

Tip

Buy anchovy paste because it can be stored refrigerated up to 3 months to use on pizzas or in tomato sauces. If you can only find canned anchovies then freeze the whole thing in a resealable freezer bag. One or two minutes on the counter will thaw these oily fishes enough to pick a single one out of the can as you need it.

1/2 cup (125 mL) silken tofu
2 tbsp (30 mL) grated
   Parmesan cheese (approx)
2 tbsp (30 mL) lemon juice
2 dashes Worcestershire
   sauce
1 clove garlic, minced

2 dashes Tabasco sauce
1 tbsp (15 mL) extra-virgin
   olive oil
1 tbsp (15 mL) white wine
   vinegar

1 tsp (5 mL) mashed
   anchovies or anchovy
   paste
Salt and pepper to taste
1 head romaine lettuce
3 slices cooked bacon
   (optional)

- In bowl, mash together tofu, Parmesan cheese, lemon juice, Worcestershire sauce, garlic, Tabasco sauce, oil, vinegar, anchovies, salt and pepper. Let sit for 1 hour. (Can be stored In fridge for up to 1 week. Dressing does not freeze well.)

- Clean, dry and tear lettuce into pieces. (Roll in paper towel and store in plastic bag until ready to use.)

- Toss salad with dressing; top with cooked bacon and extra Parmesan cheese if desired.

Grab and Go

Barbecue Chicken Caesar Salad: Though there is tofu in the dressing as protein, adding a few ounces of chicken will make this salad into an even more substantial meal. Thaw some boneless skinless chicken breasts in the microwave until soft throughout and starting to cook. Pour some barbecue sauce on the chicken and broil for 4 minutes per side until chicken is no longer pink inside. Slice into strips; arrange over Caesar salad.

Lemony Baked Shrimp

SERVES
4

PREPARATION TIME
8 MINUTES

Fresh parsley can be stored in a glass of water in the refrigerator up to ten days. You can put it out on the table so anyone can pick a leaf and sprinkle it on their dinner. When it starts to dry out, then help it dry all the way by spreading on a cookie sheet and baking in 200°F (100°C) oven for an hour or so. Store as you would any other spice in the cupboard up to 6 months.

The peel-and-eat aspect of shrimp doesn't appeal to everyone so be sure to buy shrimp that is peeled but frozen raw if your family does not like peeling. This is a good recipe for the adult meal after the kids have their grilled cheeses before soccer practice. But they will love sitting and having some noodles with you.

You can substitute 2 lb (1 kg) of halibut, cut into 2-inch (5 cm) cubes, for the shrimp. Do not mix with the remaining ingredients until just before baking because the tenderness of the fish can't take the acid of the lemon and will get mushy.

Serve with Poppy Seed Noodles (page 80). This is a non-vegetarian option for this week. Vegetarians can eat the Protein Poppy Seed Noodles (see Grab and Go, page 80).

Vegetable oil cooking spray
2 lb (1 kg) frozen medium raw shrimp, peeled and deveined

3/4 cup (175 mL) dry bread crumbs
2 tbsp (30 mL) finely chopped fresh parsley
1 tsp (5 mL) grated lemon rind

1/2 tsp (2 mL) salt
6 cloves garlic, minced
1/4 cup (50 mL) lemon juice
4 tsp (20 mL) olive oil

• Coat 4 individual gratin dishes with cooking spray. Divide shrimp among dishes.

• In bowl, combine bread crumbs, parsley, lemon rind, salt and garlic; stir in lemon juice and oil. Sprinkle evenly over shrimp. (Refrigerate up to 6 hours.)

• Bake in 400°F (200°C) oven for 15 to 30 minutes (shrimp will take up to 30 minutes if cooked from frozen, or as little as 15 minutes if thawed in refrigerator) or until shrimp are pink and opaque.

Asian Sprout and Red Pepper Salad

SERVES
4+4

This is a colourful and simple addition to any meal. Serve with Lemony Baked Shrimp (page 82).

PREPARATION TIME
10 MINUTES

**1/4 cup (50 mL) low-sodium
    soy sauce**
**1/4 cup (50 mL) toasted
    sesame oil**

**2 tbsp (30 mL) grated
    gingerroot**
**2 tbsp (30 mL) rice wine
    vinegar**

4 cups (1 L) bean sprouts
**1 sweet red pepper, thinly
    sliced or grated**

• In small bowl, whisk together soy sauce, sesame oil, ginger and vinegar; set aside.

• Rinse sprouts very well under cold running water. Drain well and place in bowl. Add dressing and red pepper; toss to coat well. (Can be refrigerated up to 3 weeks.)

Grab and Go
Tofu Sprout Salad: Cube some firm tofu and toss with extra sprout salad. Let sit to marinate at least 1 hour before serving. This is a nice light meal for a hot day.

Week 9 Shopping List

YOU NEED:

Frozen shrimp, medium, raw, peeled
  (2 lb/1 kg)
Frozen peas (1 cup/250 mL)
Frozen corn (1 cup/250 mL)
Tomato juice (2 cups/500 mL)
Cooked bacon (3 slices), optional
*Boneless skinless chicken breasts
  (1 lb/500 g)
Lemon juice (3/4 cup/175 mL)
Grated lemon rind (1 tsp/5 mL)
Red potatoes (2)
Grated Parmesan cheese
  (2 tbsp/30 mL)
Silken tofu (1/2 cup/125 mL
  + *2 cups/500 mL)
*Firm tofu (1 cup/250 mL cubed)
Carrots (4)
Green pepper (half)
Red peppers (1 1/2)
Celery (2 stalks)
Romaine lettuce (1 head)
Gingerroot (2 tbsp/30 mL grated)
Garlic (9 cloves)
Leek (1)
Onions (3)
Fresh parsley (2 tbsp/30 mL finely
  chopped)
Bean sprouts (4 cups/1 L)

CHECK YOUR PANTRY FOR:

Dry bread crumbs (3/4 cup/175 mL)
Anchovy paste (1 tsp/5 mL)
Pesto sauce (3 tbsp/45 mL)
Canned chopped stewed tomatoes
  (3 cups/750 mL)
Canned mixed beans
  (1 can, 19 oz/540 mL)
Worcestershire sauce (2 dashes)
*Barbecue sauce (1/4 cup/50 mL)
Tabasco sauce (2 dashes)
Extra-virgin olive oil (1 tbsp/15 mL)
Olive oil (4 tsp/20 mL)
Canola oil (2 tsp/10 mL)
Vegetable oil cooking spray
White wine vinegar (1 tbsp/15 mL)
Dried red lentils (2 cups/500 mL)
Low-sodium soy sauce (1/4 cup/50 mL)
Egg noodles (2 cups/500 mL)
Molasses (3 tbsp/45 mL)
Vegetable stock (3 cups/750 mL)
Dried oregano (1 tbsp/15 mL)
Chicken stock (8 cups/2 L)
Poppy seeds (1 tbsp/15 mL)
Rice wine vinegar (2 tbsp/30 mL)
Toasted sesame oil (1/3 cup/75 mL)

*grab and go items

Notes

WEEK 10

I meet a lot of parents who worry that their kids eat like birds. "Just wait," I tell them. Kids don't need a lot of calories to get through the day when they are little, and, if they know how to say "no" when they are full (instead of listening to your urging them to clean their plates), they will be well prepared for the battle against adult indulgence.

Of course, there is some singing that goes on in the heart when you see a kid hunker down to a good meal. When they are truly hungry and there is no stopping them, be sure to have good food ready. They will blast through your kitchen like the Tasmanian devil. We used to watch my nephew at about age 12 eat cereal from a salad bowl. He could down a box of shredded wheat in two days. We could not keep our place stocked with enough food when he was around. And then his friends would come over! Now at over six feet tall he can still out-eat his dad, but he's a healthy, strapping example of good food in, good kid out.

In one cooking class, I had a preteen along with the others, who were aged seven to nine. The younger ones began to insist that we put his portion of our just-cooked food on a separate plate, because he could demolish the platter before any of them could even reach it.

Your kids will eat—eventually. Focusing on lifelong habits rather than the number of corn niblets ingested helps. And keeping the teenagers at the back of the line at any family function will be something you'll have to get used to soon enough.

Super Bowl Sunday and Munchies All Week Long

Lower-Fat Chili Con Carne

✽Souvlaki Pork with Tossed Greek Salad

Chicken Stuffed with Sun-Dried Tomatoes and Chèvre

Quinoa and Carrots

WORK SCHEDULE

1 Sauté ground beef for Lower-Fat Chili Con Carne while you wash and prepare veggies for the chili and the souvlaki.
2 Drain and complete chili recipe once you have removed all vegetables from the sink.
3 Chop and marinate pork for souvlaki for 4 to 8 hours and serve tonight.
4 Chop veggies for Tossed Greek Salad. Make dip.
5 Assemble Chicken Stuffed with Sun-Dried Tomatoes and Chèvre.
6 Quinoa and Carrots can be prepared on the day you cook the Chicken Stuffed with Sun-Dried Tomatoes and Chèvre.

✽Serve it tonight.

Lower-Fat Chili Con Carne

SERVES
4+4

PREPARATION TIME
20 MINUTES

Leftover tomato paste is a pain to store but if you cut open the top and bottom of the can leaving cut ends in place and then wrap in plastic wrap and freeze the can, it becomes a whole new convenience food. Since you only use a spoonful or two at a time, you can thaw slightly under hot running water and press the bottom lid up to expose some frozen paste. Use a sharp, hot knife to slice off the amount you need. Each centimetre is about 1 tbsp (15 mL).

Many kids will eat chili without the beans, so simply add beans only to the adult portions.

Running hot water over cooked ground beef takes extra fat out. Adding lots of vegetables updates this family pleaser.

1 lb (500 g) medium ground beef
2 cups (500 mL) chopped onion
2 stalks celery, chopped
1 sweet green pepper, seeded, cored and chopped

2 tbsp (30 mL) finely minced garlic
2 tbsp (30 mL) chili powder
1 tsp (5 mL) dried oregano
1 tsp (5 mL) ground cumin
1/4 tsp (1 mL) pepper
1 bay leaf
1 can (6 oz/180 mL) unsalted tomato paste

2 cups (500 mL) canned chopped tomatoes
3/4 cup (175 mL) water
1 tbsp (15 mL) red wine vinegar
1 can (19 oz/540 mL) red kidney beans, drained
1 tbsp (15 mL) Chili Spice (page 139)

• In large deep pot, sauté beef until no longer pink. Pour into colander and drain off fat. Run hot water over meat; let sit in sink to remove even more fat.

• Add onion, celery and green pepper to pot; cook until onion is translucent, 6 to 8 minutes. Add garlic, chili powder, oregano, cumin, pepper and bay leaf; stir for 1 minute. Return meat to pan; add tomato paste, canned tomatoes, water and vinegar. Bring to boil; reduce heat and simmer 15 minutes. Stir in beans; simmer 15 minutes. Remove bay leaf before serving. Stir in Chili Spice. (Freeze in single-serving sizes up to 6 weeks.)

Grab and Go

Burritos: Chili is a great, versatile meal. Try to find soft corn wraps: they have a dense texture that is crispy when baked. Oil a casserole dish and lay a corn tortilla on the bottom. Warm some chili and spread on top. Place a second tortilla on top and spread with some salsa or more chili. Lay the third layer and sprinkle with shredded cheese. This can sit in the refrigerator for up to 2 days. Bake 30 to 45 minutes in a 350°F (180°C) oven, uncovered. Serve like a pizza and slice into triangles.

Better Spaghetti Sauce – Week 1

Chicken Cacciatore – Week 3

Baked Pork Tenderloin with Spinach and Blue Cheese – Week 3

Salmon with Spinach and Feta in Parchment – Week 6

Tuna Sailboats for Kids – Week 8

Roast Beef with Rosemary and Garlic Veggies – Week 8

French Toast – Breakfast Plan 1

Souvlaki Pork with Tossed Greek Salad

Serve this with a mixed green salad and whole wheat pita pockets.

Souvlaki:
2 lb (1 kg) pork tenderloin
1/4 cup (50 mL) olive oil
1 clove garlic
1 tsp (5 mL) dried oregano
Salt to taste
Half lemon

Salad:
1 cucumber
1 sweet red pepper
3 stalks celery
1/2 cup (125 mL) black olives

Dressing/Dip:
2 cups (500 mL) plain yogurt
1/4 cup (50 mL) crumbled
   feta cheese
1 tbsp (15 mL) honey Dijon
   mustard
1 tsp (5 mL) garlic powder
1 tsp (5 mL) dried oregano
Salt to taste

SERVES
4+4

PREPARATION TIME
15 MINUTES

If your kids are very particular about foods touching each other then lay the salad out on a platter and cover with plastic wrap. Leave olives in a separate dish for adults to enjoy.

- Souvlaki: Cut pork into 2-inch (5 cm) cubes; place in large resealable freezer bag. Add oil, garlic, oregano and salt. Squeeze lemon half into bag; add rind. Seal bag and shake. Refrigerate to marinate up to 24 hours. (Meat can be frozen up to 3 weeks: thaw in refrigerator.)

- Salad: Cut cucumber, red pepper and celery into cubes; toss together with olives.

- Dressing/Dip: In bowl, mix yogurt, feta cheese, Dijon mustard, garlic powder, oregano and salt. Serve as dip or toss with cucumber mixture.

- Arrange pork in single layer in roasting pan; bake in 450°F (230°C) oven for 16 to 18 minutes until just a hint of pink remains inside. Broil for 1 to 2 minutes to brown.

Grab and Go

Pork Picnic: Once the pork is cooked, you can freeze it to serve as an appetizer at a fireside supper or an eat-on-the-run finger food with some carrot and celery sticks. Freeze it for up to 3 weeks and thaw in the fridge. Serve cold or warm in microwave on defrost setting for a very few minutes.

Chicken Stuffed with Sun-Dried Tomatoes and Chèvre

SERVES
4+4

PREPARATION TIME
18 MINUTES

Food, like fashion, has its time. But some things last: the 1980s pairing of tomatoes and chèvre has become a timeless classic. Delicious!

10 sun-dried tomatoes packed in oil	2 cloves garlic, minced	Salt and pepper to taste
1 tbsp (15 mL) light mayonnaise (optional)	6 oz (175 g) chèvre	8 (3 lb/1.5 kg) boneless skinless chicken breasts
	1 tsp (5 mL) crumbled dried rosemary	

You can also use dry-packed tomatoes. Place in microwaveable dish. Cover with water and microwave at high for 5 minutes; drain and chop.

- Chop tomatoes roughly.
- In bowl, mix together mayonnaise if using, tomatoes, garlic, chèvre, rosemary, salt and pepper.
- Pat chicken dry with paper towels. Lay out 4 large pieces of plastic wrap about 18 inches (45 cm) long; place 2 breasts on each. Scoop about 1 tbsp (15 mL) cheese mixture onto each breast. Fold breasts around cheese mixture envelope-style and turn over. Smear remaining cheese mixture on each breast. Wrap plastic around each pair. Place packages in large resealable freezer bag. (Store in freezer up to 3 weeks.)
- In plastic wrap, partially precook 4 breasts in microwave for 10 to 15 minutes at high. Remove plastic wrap and place in baking dish, leaving space between each.
- Bake in 350°F (180°C) oven for 25 to 35 minutes or until no longer pink inside.

Grab and Go

Chèvre and Chicken Soup: In saucepan, bring 4 cups (1 L) chicken stock with 2 cups (500 mL) water to boil. Add 2 new potatoes, scrubbed and chopped into small pieces, and 1 tsp (5 mL) dried thyme; simmer until potatoes are tender. Using hand blender, purée until smooth; add chopped cooked chicken and return to boil. Reduce heat and simmer until chicken is warmed through, 2 to 3 minutes. Add some milk to thin to desired consistency but do not boil or it will separate. Add salt and pepper to taste and top with more chèvre if you like.

Quinoa and Carrots

SERVES
4

This is a great side dish the day you cook your chicken.

PREPARATION TIME
4 MINUTES

2 cups (500 mL) water or chicken stock	**2 cups (500 mL) frozen sliced carrots**	**Salt and pepper to taste**
1 cup (250 mL) quinoa	**1 tbsp (15 mL) butter**	

- In large pot, bring water to boil. Add quinoa; cook for 10 minutes until quinoa breaks up a bit.
- Meanwhile, microwave carrots just to thaw. Add to quinoa; simmer 2 to 5 minutes until softened and warmed through. Stir in butter, salt and pepper. (Refrigerate up to 24 hours.)

Quinoa is one of the less used grains but it has more magnesium, zinc, copper and iron than brown rice and cooks in a third of the time. Once you try this teeny weenie powerhouse with butter, you will get over its weird name, which is pronounced keenwa.

If you want to skip the new grain or just could not find it at the grocery store, substitute any pasta, but the size from Week 5 would be just fine.

Week 10 Shopping List

YOU NEED:

Chèvre (6 oz/175 g)
*Corn tortillas (1 pkg)
Whole wheat pita bread (1 pkg)
*Shredded cheese, any kind
   (2 cups/500 mL)
Feta cheese (1/4 cup/50 mL)
Plain yogurt (2 cups/500 mL)
Frozen sliced carrots (2 cups/500 mL)
Quinoa (1 cup/250 mL)
Pork tenderloin (2 lb/1 kg)
Medium ground beef (1 lb/500 g)
Boneless skinless chicken breasts, 8
   (3 lb/1.5 kg)
Sun-dried tomatoes (10)
Red pepper (1)
Green pepper (1)
Onions (3)
Garlic (10 cloves)
Cucumber (1)
Celery (5 stalks)
Mixed greens (1 pkg)
Lemon (half)
*New potatoes (2)

CHECK YOUR PANTRY FOR:

Black olives (1/2 cup/125 mL)
Canned chopped tomatoes
   (1 can, 19 oz/540 mL)
Red kidney beans (1 can, 19 oz/540 mL)
*Salsa (1 jar)
Honey Dijon mustard (1 tbsp/15 mL)
Light mayonnaise (1 tbsp/15 mL),
   optional
Olive oil (1/4 cup/50 mL)
Butter (1 tbsp/15 mL)
*Frozen chicken stock (6 cups/1.5 L)
Bay leaf (1)
Chili powder (2 tbsp/30 mL)
Dried rosemary (1 tsp/5 mL)
Dried oregano (1 tbsp/15 mL)
*Dried thyme (1 tsp/5 mL)
Garlic powder (1 tsp/5 mL)
Ground cumin (1 tsp/5 mL)
Unsalted tomato paste
   (1 can, 6 oz/180 mL can)
Red wine vinegar (1 tbsp/15 mL)

*grab and go items

Notes

WEEK 11

The last two weeks of this book contain more sophisticated recipes for older, more adventurous palates, paying special attention to fish. Adding fish to any diet is an important shift to make for overall health, but especially for the growing brains and bodies of teenagers. There are many schools of thought around fish these days, but the general consensus is that the benefits of fresh or farmed fish still far outweigh the potential negatives of contamination. I suppose you get to choose your poison: the heart-healthy lean protein with omega-3 brain builders now versus the possible effects of toxins later. The best way to handle this issue is to spread out your consumption. Most experts agree that you can eat fish up to three times per week without any harm being done while reaping huge benefits. Educate yourself about where your fish comes from and try to vary the types you eat. Switch it up a bit from deep ocean fish to lake fish to bivalves and crustaceans. A wide variety ensures that you get good nutrients and reduces the risk of build-up of any one kind of toxin from one area.

Here are my top picks: Salmon, either farmed or wild—enjoy it in moderation for its omega-3 goodness. Shrimp and scallops are a great protein to add to any pasta sauce or soup right out of the freezer. Canned clams make an amazing, lean protein addition to soups. Choose Pacific sole when you are looking for a mild, quick-cooking fish (Atlantic sole is over-fished). Rainbow trout is best straight up and fried in butter because it is a tender lake fish with good omega-3 counts. Canned tuna is the perennial favourite for its ease. Lobster (for special occasions only since its mercury levels can be high) is just oh, so good.

Grown-Up Kids of All Ages

*Balsamic Barley Salad

Southwestern Fish Sticks

*Creamy Baked Salmon

Guacamole

Bistro Burgers

WORK SCHEDULE

1 Simmer barley for Balsamic Barley Salad. Turn off when cooked; complete later.
2 Assemble fish sticks and freeze.
3 Prepare the salmon and store in fridge until you are ready to prepare supper for tonight.
4 Mix the Guacamole and store in freezer.
5 Complete Balsamic Barley Salad and store in fridge, covered, until you are ready to serve tonight.
6 Make the burgers last to avoid spreading any bacteria from raw meat; freeze. Skip croutons until the day you are serving the burgers.

---

*Serve it tonight.

Balsamic Barley Salad

SERVES
10

PREPARATION TIME
11 MINUTES

Bags of pot barley are sold by weight so the amount will vary. Simply use the whole bag and adjust the liquid upward as necessary.

Never underestimate the power of the frozen vegetable! It is often more nutritious than its fresh counterpart, which may have travelled and been improperly stored for many days. Thawed frozen corn mixed with salsa is a great dip for corn chips.

Spend a few extra dollars on a good bottle of balsamic vinegar. It is much less acidic than the less expensive kind and the difference is noticeable.

2–2 1/2 (500–625 mL) cups pot barley
3 cups (750 mL) water
2 cups (500 mL) beef stock
1 cup (250 mL) frozen corn

1 cup (250 mL) frozen green beans
1 cup (250 mL) frozen peas
1/2 cup (125 mL) balsamic vinegar

1/4 cup (50 mL) extra-virgin olive oil
2 tbsp (30 mL) soy sauce
Salt and pepper to taste

• In very large pot, bring barley, water and stock to boil. Reduce heat and simmer for 40 minutes until barley is chewable. Turn off heat even though there may still be some water to absorb.

• Break green beans into barley while still warm. Add corn and peas; stir. Add vinegar, oil, soy sauce, salt and pepper. Cover and let stand until cool. Empty into serving bowl and cover with plastic wrap.

Grab and Go
Barley Salad with Cottage Cheese and Greens: There will be lots of barley salad made with this recipe and it will keep in the fridge for up to 5 days. Serve it with everything. Some lettuce and a mound of barley salad with a mound of cottage cheese makes a nice light, complex carbohydrate and protein meal that is loaded with fibre.

Southwestern Fish Sticks

Serve with plum sauce and Guacamole (page 98) as well as some frozen corn that has been warmed in the microwave. The addition of a mixed green salad makes this a light and nourishing meal full of good fats and brain food.

1 cup (250 mL) yellow cornmeal	2 tbsp (30 mL) chili powder	1/2 tsp (2 mL) white pepper
2/3 cup (150 mL) Italian seasoned bread crumbs	1 tbsp (15 mL) ground cumin	2 lb (1 kg) Pacific cod fillets (or Pacific haddock)
1/2 cup (125 mL) grated Parmesan cheese	1 tbsp (15 mL) garlic powder	1/2 cup (125 mL) milk
	1 tsp (5 mL) granulated sugar	1/4 cup (50 mL) plum sauce
	1 tsp (5 mL) hot pepper flakes	

- In large resealable plastic bag, combine cornmeal, bread crumbs, Parmesan, chili powder, cumin, garlic powder, sugar, chili flakes and white pepper; shake well.
- Line baking sheet small enough to fit into freezer with foil; spray with cooking spray.
- Rinse fish under cold water; slice into 3- x 1/2-inch (8 x 1 cm) sticks. In another freezer bag, mix plum sauce with milk; add fish and gently toss to coat. Place 3 or 4 fish fingers at a time into cornmeal mixture and shake gently. Place on baking sheet; spray top of each. Freeze 2 to 4 hours; remove to resealable plastic bag. (Can be frozen for up to 3 weeks.)
- Place desired number of frozen fish sticks on baking sheet. Bake in 375°F (190°C) oven for 20 to 35 minutes until firm and slightly browned.

Grab and Go

Fish Sticks and Sweet Potato Fries: There are enough fish sticks here to serve four people twice. Try serving them a different way the second time. Slice 3 sweet potatoes lengthwise and then into wedges. Toss with 1/4 cup (50 mL) olive oil and lay out on a baking sheet. Bake in 450°F (230°C) oven for 15 minutes before you add the fish sticks on their baking sheet. Ketchup is the dip of choice here!

SERVES
8

PREPARATION TIME
20 MINUTES

Plum sauce, although sweet, actually has some minor nutrient value. Not from the plums, but from the pumpkin purée that is often added to make the sauce orange. Who knew?

Cornmeal makes an awesome side dish. In the south, it's called grits but in Italy it is polenta. Either way, this whole grain pasta substitute is simple. Simmer 3 parts water with 1 part cornmeal for 15 minutes, stirring often. Add water as needed. Stir in generous amounts of salt and pepper as well as a tablespoon or two (15 to 30 mL) of butter at the end of the cooking time and call it grits. Or press leftovers into a cake or loaf pan to be cut into squares and pan-fried in olive oil and call it polenta. Top it with Parmesan cheese.

I have specified Pacific cod here only because Atlantic cod tends to be overfished and we need to think about our planet as well as our plate.

Guacamole

SERVES
12

Avocados are one my favourite fruits, full of flavour and good fats.

| 3 green onions, trimmed
6 ripe avocados | 1 tbsp (15 mL) relish
1 tsp (5 mL) dried thyme | 3 tbsp (45 mL) fresh lime
juice |

PREPARATION TIME
15 MINUTES

Tip

Storing cut avocado is tricky because the flesh browns so quickly, but if you spray the cut side with cooking spray lightly before wrapping and refrigerating, your avocado should stay green.

- Using hand blender or mini chopper, finely mince green onions, including fair bit of green parts to keep dip green during freezing.
- Slice avocados in half; squeeze out pit and flesh into bowl. Discard pit and skin. Add relish and thyme to flesh; mash with fork to leave a few chunks or use hand blender to purée. Add green onions and half of the lime juice, stir.
- Empty into 3 ramekins or small serving dishes; pour remaining lime juice over tops. Cover tightly with plastic wrap and freeze up to 2 weeks. To serve, remove from freezer at least 2 hours before serving to thaw. Serve with blue corn tortilla chips, or Southwestern Fish Sticks.

Creamy Baked Salmon

SERVES
4

Evaporated milk makes this dish creamy without the fat. Add some mixed greens and serve with Balsamic Barley Salad (page 96).

| 1 lb (500 g) salmon fillets
1 tsp (5 mL) dried tarragon | 1/4 tsp (1 mL) salt
Pepper to taste | 1 can (8 oz/225 mL)
evaporated skim milk |

PREPARATION TIME
15 MINUTES

Tip

Asian sesame oil comes in two forms: toasted or light. The toasted or dark version is what we are looking for when we want to add that Asian flavour. Its amber colour comes from the seeds being toasted, which brings out their nutty flavour.

- Rinse salmon under cold water and pat dry with paper towel. Lay salmon in large shallow ceramic or glass baking dish. Sprinkle with tarragon, salt and pepper; pour evaporated milk over top. (Ideally, the dish is large enough that the salmon is only half submerged.) Cover with plastic wrap and refrigerate up to 8 hours.
- Bake, uncovered, in 400°F (200°C) oven for 10 to 12 minutes, basting twice, until fish flakes easily when tested with fork.

Grab and Go

Asian Salmon Sandwich: Mash leftover salmon and liquid with 1 tsp (5 mL) toasted sesame oil, 1 tbsp (15 mL) honey mustard, 1 tsp (5 mL) soy sauce and 1/2 tsp (2 mL) grated gingerroot. Place on whole wheat burger bun and top with 1/2 cup (125 mL) grated cabbage. Some extra grated cabbage on the side sprinkled with toasted sesame oil and soy sauce makes for a high-fibre, delicious side dish.

Bistro Burgers

Here's a versatile mixture of beef and flavourings that can become either burgers or meatballs.

2 cups (500 mL) sliced
  mushrooms
2 cups (500 mL) red wine or
  beef stock
8 slices (1/2 inch/1 cm thick)
  whole grain bread
2 tbsp (30 mL) Italian herb
  seasoning

1 pkg (10 oz/280 g) fresh
  baby spinach
2 cups (500 mL) cherry
  tomatoes
Burgers:
4 green onions
2 lb (1 kg) extra-lean
  ground beef

1/2 cup (125 mL) dry Italian
  seasoned bread crumbs
2 eggs
2 tsp (10 mL) dried thyme
Salt and pepper to taste

SERVES
8

PREPARATION TIME
10 MINUTES

To make quick, plain burgers, simply broil for 15 to 20 minutes.

The dimple in the patty fills in as meat cooks and shrinks and prevents the meat from expanding in the middle, causing it to be raw due to thickness.

If you want to omit the bread altogether, add the Italian herbs to the wine jus for added flavour.

- Lay out 4 pieces of foil about 12 inches (30 cm) long.
- Burgers: Finely mince green onions; place in large bowl. Add beef, bread crumbs, eggs, thyme, salt and pepper; mix well with hands. Divide into 8; form each into 4-inch (10 cm) diameter patty, pressing firmly. Press a dimple with thumb into centre of each. Place 2 patties on each piece of foil and wrap loosely; place in resealable plastic bag and freeze up to 1 month.
- Heat nonstick pan with lid. Brown frozen burgers on each side, remove and pat dry with paper towel. Add mushrooms; stir for 6 to 8 minutes. Place burgers on mushrooms; pour in red wine or stock (or combo of both). Cover and simmer 20 minutes or until meat thermometer inserted sideways registers 160°F (70°C).
- Lay bread on baking sheet; spray bread with cooking spray. Sprinkle with herbs; broil for 1 to 2 minutes each side (watch carefully).
- Top each with burger; pour some wine jus with mushrooms over top. Serve with spinach and cherry tomatoes.

Grab and Go

Meatballs: If you think that one burger meal is all you will eat within a month, try rolling half of this mixture into meatballs about 1 inch (2.5 cm) in diameter. Bake on baking sheet in 375°F (190°C) oven for 25 to 35 minutes. They're great to add to pasta sauce. Or add to barbecue sauce and reheat in microwave. Toothpick meals are always a good idea for those freaky days in June or September that are actually hot.

Week 11 Shopping List

YOU NEED:

*Whole wheat hamburger buns (8)
Whole grain bread (1 loaf)
Eggs (2)
Milk (1/2 cup/125 mL)
Grated Parmesan cheese
   (1/2 cup/125 mL)
*Cottage cheese (2 cups/500 mL)
Pacific cod fillets (2 lb/1 kg)
Salmon fillets (1 lb/500 g)
Extra-lean ground beef (2 lb/1 kg)
Frozen green beans (1 cup/250 mL)
Frozen corn (1 cup/250 mL)
Frozen peas (1 cup/250 mL)
*Mixed greens (2 pkg, 10 oz/300 g
   each)
Baby spinach (1 pkg, 10 oz/280 g)
Mushrooms (6 oz/180 g)
Cherry tomatoes (2 cups/500 mL)
*Grated cabbage (1 pkg)
*Sweet potatoes (3)
Avocados (6)
Green onions (1 bunch)
Gingerroot (1/2 tsp/2 mL grated)

CHECK YOUR PANTRY FOR:

Italian seasoned bread crumbs
   (1 1/3 cups/325 mL)
Evaporated skim milk (1 can, 8 oz/225 mL)
Red wine (2 cups/500 mL)
Soy sauce (2 tbsp/30 mL)
*Barbecue sauce (1 cup/250 mL)
*Toasted sesame oil (1 tbsp/15 mL)
*Honey mustard (1 tbsp/15 mL)
Extra-virgin olive oil (1/4 cup/50 mL)
Olive oil (1/4 cup/50 mL)
Yellow cornmeal (1 cup/250 mL)
Pot barley (2 1/2 cups/625 mL)
Relish (1 tbsp/15 mL)
Lime juice (3 tbsp/45 mL)
Blue corn tortilla chips (1 pkg)
Beef stock (2 cups/500 mL)
Dried thyme (1 tbsp/15 mL)
Garlic powder (1 tbsp/15 mL)
White pepper (1/2 tsp/2 mL)
Dried tarragon (1 tsp/5 mL)
Chili powder (2 tbsp/30 mL)
Hot pepper flakes (1 tsp/5 mL)
Italian herb seasoning (2 tbsp/30 mL)
Ground cumin (1 tbsp/15 mL)
Plum sauce (1/4 cup/50 mL)
Balsamic vinegar (1/2 cup/125 mL)

*grab and go items

Notes

WEEK 12

Whether I entertain two ladies for lunch or an entire family of fussies, I like to sit with my guests. I feel so sad when I see a host slaving over details when her guests really want to catch up with her. What a shame that the cook does all the work and then sits down, exhausted, at 11 p.m. when everyone is ready to leave!

Because I do what I do for a living, everyone expects that when they come to my house they will be well fed. This doesn't mean that I do everything myself. Once in a while, I will get the urge to make my own salsa, but most of the time the best bottle I can find will do.

The best advice I can give a host is to plan everything in advance, spend time on the presentation and cut corners everywhere else. The concept of "good enough" is hard to convey but any one-pot dish served in a soup tureen sprinkled with fresh herbs is pretty easy to do. Homemade biscuits make it special, but you could buy those from a good bakery instead. Roll a cold stick of butter in some chopped herbs, and it looks like you worked all day. Take time with your table and create something unique. Serving salad in lovely little flowerpots makes more of an impression than toiling over the dressing to get the acid balance just right. Use one interesting ingredient, a prickly pear for instance, and you've got dinnertime conversation started.

Best advice I ever got? Never apologize, never explain. If you adhere to this next time you burn the vegetables, your guests will think you invented a new dish: Blackened Green Beans!

Unique Tastes

Sesame Fish Cakes with Baby Bok Choy

*Scallops and Soy Beans in Sake Stock

Thai Stuffed Pork with Mashed Apples and Squash

Spicy Coconut Salad

WORK SCHEDULE

1 Start the Sesame Fish Cakes first and let the potatoes cook.
2 Wash and assemble the ingredients for the Scallops and Soy Beans in Sake Stock; set on counter or in fridge. Cooking tonight will take only 10 minutes.
3 Make the stuffing for Thai Stuffed Pork; stuff and refrigerate. (Do not prepare Mashed Apples and Squash until the day you are serving.)
4 Make the salad dressing; toss just before serving.

---

*Serve it tonight.

Sesame Fish Cakes with Baby Bok Choy

SERVES
8

PREPARATION TIME
30 MINUTES

You could use any mild white fish in this recipe. Try tilapia, it is the mildest, and so far has safe mercury levels as well as a moderate omega-3 count. This species is, at the moment, not overfished. Other options include Pacific sole (Atlantic is overfished), rainbow trout or Pacific cod.

6 thin-skinned potatoes (Yukon Gold or white)
6 frozen white fish fillets, thawed
2 green onions
1/2 cup (125 mL) chopped fresh parsley

1 tbsp (15 mL) grated gingerroot
4 cloves garlic, minced
1 tbsp (15 mL) salt
Coating:
1/4 cup (50 mL) cornmeal
1/4 cup (50 mL) sesame seeds

1 tbsp (15 mL) curry powder
Baby Bok Choy:
4 baby bok choy
2 tbsp (30 mL) seasoned rice vinegar
1 jar (8 oz/236 mL) sweet chili sauce

- Scrub (but do not peel) potatoes; chop into quarters. In large pot of boiling water, cook potatoes for 15 minutes until soft enough to be poked with knife. Add fish; simmer for 2 to 4 minutes until fish flakes easily when tested with fork.

- Meanwhile, rinse green onions under cold running water. Chop, then place in large bowl; add parsley, ginger, garlic and salt.

- Coating: On plate, mix cornmeal, sesame seeds and curry powder; set aside. Drain fish mixture. (Set aside any children's portions that you wish to keep plain to roll in plain cornmeal and salt and freeze with the seasoned ones.) Add potatoes and fish to green onion mixture; mash with potato masher or hand blender until soft but not smooth. Let cool.

- Spray 3 or 4 large pieces of foil with cooking spray.

- Form potato mixture by 1/2 cupfuls (125 mL) into patties. Roll in cornmeal mixture and place on foil; spray tops with cooking spray and fold foil over. Freeze up to 3 weeks.

- Spray large skillet with cooking spray; heat over medium-high heat. Brown 3 or 4 patties at a time on one side before turning carefully. Cover to allow to warm through, turning once more. Reduce heat to medium-low.

- Meanwhile, pull leaves apart and rinse baby bok choy. Place in large microwaveable bowl; sprinkle with rice vinegar and toss with sweet chili sauce. Cover and microwave at high for 4 to 6 minutes just to soften. Serve with fish cakes.

Grab and Go (A slow-cooker is the family's best friend.)

Easy Fish Chowder: Place 4 frozen fish cakes in slow-cooker; add 4 to 6 cups (1 to 1.5 L) chicken stock. Cook on low for 3 to 4 hours. Add 2 cups (500 mL) frozen corn and 1 can (16 oz/540 mL) baby clams, undrained. Stir in some cream; drizzle with sherry.

Scallops and Soy Beans in Sake Stock

SERVES
4

PREPARATION TIME
10 MINUTES

This is a very light meal, great for hot evenings when you don't feel like making a big fuss. Serve in large pasta bowls with rice crackers on the side.

2 tbsp (30 mL) olive oil
1 pkg (14 oz/400 g) frozen
   scallops, thawed
2 cups (500 mL) sake (or
   1 cup/250 mL white wine)

2 cups (500 mL) chicken
   stock
2 cups (500 mL) frozen soy
   beans, shelled

1 tbsp (15 mL) chili sauce
   (approx)
1/2 lb (225 g) rapini, rinsed
   well and trimmed

- In large skillet, heat oil. Brown scallops slightly then flip. (Remove any children's portions to serve as is; cover with foil and let stand on stove to keep warm and continue cooking.)
- Pour sake and chicken stock over scallops; bring to boil. Simmer for 5 minutes. Add soy beans and chili sauce. Lay rapini over scallops and baste with liquid. Place entire skillet on broiler rack 4 inches (10 cm) from heat; broil for 2 to 6 minutes until warmed through.

Frozen soy beans are a great source of protein and are simple to prepare. If you can purchase the already-shelled beans, all they need is a quick steam for 4 to 5 minutes and some salt or soy sauce and they are a great snack or side dish.

Rapini is the bitter cousin of broccoli, not because it gets chosen less often but because its flavour is much stronger. All it needs is a quick steam on the stovetop or microwave. Try chopping it into smaller pieces and sprinkling with sugar, balsamic vinegar, olive oil and Parmesan cheese. This Italian vegetable can hold its own served with any strong meat like ribs or beef.

Thai Stuffed Pork with Mashed Apples and Squash

SERVES
6+4

PREPARATION TIME
18 MINUTES

The peanuty flavours with fresh basil are reminiscent of Thailand and the side dish is a snap.

2 cups (500 mL) matzo meal	4 1 lb (500 g) pork tender- loins, butterflied	**Mashed Apples and Squash:**
1/2 cup (125 mL) bottled peanut sauce	1 bunch fresh basil, rinsed, drained and stemmed	2 cups (500 mL) frozen apple slices
1/4 cup (50 mL) water	1/4 cup (50 mL) balsamic vinegar	2 cups (500 mL) frozen squash
1 tbsp (15 mL) toasted sesame oil	2 sweet red peppers, seeded, cored and sliced	2 tbsp (30 mL) butter
1 tsp (5 mL) aniseed		1/2 tsp (2 mL) nutmeg
2 cloves garlic, minced		

- Mix together matzo meal, peanut sauce, water, sesame oil, aniseed and garlic for stuffing.

- Lay out 2 large pieces of foil. Cut 4 pieces of butcher's twine. Lay 1 butterflied tenderloin on foil; top with half of the stuffing, top with half of the basil. Place second butterflied tenderloin on top. Slide 2 pieces of twine under bottom and tie into thirds. Drizzle with balsamic vinegar, spray with cooking spray and wrap in foil. Repeat with other tenderloins. Freeze in resealable plastic bags for up to 4 weeks. Thaw in refrigerator overnight.

- Place pork on baking sheet with foil opened flat; arrange red peppers around pork. Bake in 325°F (160°C) oven for 1 hour until stuffing is hot and juices run clear when pork is pierced. Slice diagonally to keep layers intact.

- Mashed Apples and Squash: Meanwhile, in microwaveable bowl, mix apples, squash and 1/4 cup (50 mL) water; microwave on high for 15 minutes. Mash until chunky but smooth. Add butter and nutmeg. Serve with pork.

You could use any cracker that has been crushed. Try substituting melba toast or Saltines if matzo meal is hard to find.

Matzo meal is an incredibly versatile ingredient. Try making a bread pudding using it. Soak 1 cup (250 mL) matzo in 2 cups (500 mL) milk; beat 4 eggs and stir in. Add 1 cup (250 mL) raisins or any other dried fruit as well as 1/2 cup (125 mL) slivered almonds. Stir in 1 tbsp (15 mL) cinnamon and 1/2 cup (125 mL) sugar. Press into greased casserole dish; dot with butter and bake in 350°F (180°C) oven for 45 minutes.

Grab and Go

Pork and Tomato Salad: Leftover sliced pork makes a great salad the next day. Toss pork with a couple of tablespoons (30 mL) Russian salad dressing. Slice some cherry tomatoes and toss together with generous amounts of salt and pepper. Serve over a bed of mixed greens or romaine lettuce.

Spicy Coconut Salad

SERVES
6

If you have a mini chopper or mini food processor, you can make the dressing in half the time.

PREPARATION TIME
4 MINUTES

1 clove garlic, minced
Half jalapeño pepper, minced
1/4 cup (50 mL) firmly packed
   brown sugar

1/4 cup (50 mL) lime juice
1/4 cup (50 mL) coconut milk
Salt and pepper to taste

1 pkg (10 oz/300g) mixed
   fresh greens
1/4 cup (50 mL) chopped
   peanuts

Tip

- In jar with a tight-fitting lid, shake garlic, jalapeño pepper, brown sugar, lime juice and coconut milk. Add salt and pepper to taste. (Dressing can be stored in fridge up to 1 week.)
- Just before serving, toss greens with dressing and top with peanuts.

For a quick summertime meal, add 4 barbecued chicken breasts.

Week 12 Shopping List

YOU NEED:

Grated Parmesan cheese
  (1/4 cup/50 mL)
*Cream (1/4 cup/50 mL), optional
Frozen scallops (1 pkg, 400 g)
Frozen white fish fillets, sole or haddock
  (1 lb/500 g)
Pork tenderloin (4 lb/2 kg)
*Frozen corn (2 cups/500 mL)
Frozen soy beans (2 cups/500 mL)
Frozen apple slices (2 cups/500 mL)
Frozen squash (2 cups/500 mL)
Gingerroot (1 tbsp/15 mL grated)
Potatoes, Yukon Gold (6)
Fresh basil (1 bunch)
Parsley (1/2 cup/125 mL)
Rapini (1/2 lb/225 g)
Baby bok choy (4)
Red peppers (2)
*Cherry tomatoes (1 pkg)
Garlic (7 cloves)
*Mixed greens (2 pkg, 10 oz/300 g
  each)
Green onions (2)
Jalapeño pepper (half)
Lime juice (1/4 cup/50 mL)

CHECK YOUR PANTRY FOR:

Brown sugar (1/4 cup/50 mL)
Butter (2 tbsp/30 mL)
*Canned baby clams
  (1 can, 16 oz/540 mL)
*Chicken stock (8 cups/2 L)
Sweet chili sauce (1 jar, 236 mL)
Chili sauce (1 tbsp/15 mL)
Peanut sauce (1/2 cup/125 mL)
*Russian salad dressing (2 tbsp/30 mL)
Olive oil (1/4 cup/50 mL)
Toasted sesame oil (1 tbsp/15 mL)
Rice crackers (1 pkg)
Cornmeal (1/4 cup/50 mL)
Sesame seeds (1/4 cup/50 mL)
Matzo meal (2 cups/500 mL)
Curry powder (1tbsp/15 mL)
Aniseed (1 tsp/5 mL)
Nutmeg (1 tsp/2 mL)
Balsamic vinegar (1/4 cup/50 mL)
Seasoned rice vinegar (2 tbsp/30 mL)
Sake (2 cups/500 mL) or white wine
  (1 cup/250 mL)
Peanuts (1/4 cup/50 mL chopped)
Coconut milk (1/4 cup/50 mL)

*grab and go items

Notes

This is not really a full week of family meals, but rather a collection of recipes that will make even the fussiest kids happy. Make these dishes with your kids.

When my daughter was just five weeks old, I met a group of gals who would shape my life forever. The women who met every Friday for fitness and a coffee hour were mothers who had done this all before and had lots to share. I found that they were lawyers, singers, actors, docents, nurses, psychologists and others who were awe inspiring in many ways. And yet, they were all baffled about how to get meals on the table. That was the one thing I could do! They were the catalyst for my personal chef business.

In the early days, my friend up the street with little ones would often call and say, "Let's pool our resources." It meant that her husband was working late and the kids were climbing the walls. One of us would make the protein, one would make the starch, we would offer whatever veggies we had in the fridge and while away the "witching hours" between 5 and 7 p.m. Figuring out how to make that time go more smoothly, with healthier offerings, is what this week's menus are all about. I haven't met anyone who feels good about serving frozen nuggets to their kids. Having a few recipes like the Homemade Chicken Fingers in your freezer makes suppertime survival a lot easier (and even better when enjoyed with a friend).

Bonus Kids Week

*Lasagna Roll-Ups

Boston Baked Beans

Homemade Chicken Fingers

*Cucumber Faces

WORK SCHEDULE

1 Demonstrate the Lasagna Roll-Ups to kids and let them continue while you move on to the Boston Baked Beans.
2 Start Boston Baked Beans and bake for the entire day.
3 Lay roll-ups in pan; cover with cheese, wrap and refrigerate.
4 Have children combine the bread crumb mixture for the Homemade Chicken Fingers while you rinse and prepare the raw chicken. Then let them shake the chicken pieces to coat. Freeze.
5 Let kids assemble Cucumber Faces once the chicken is thoroughly cleaned from their hands.

---

*Serve it tonight.

Lasagna Roll-Ups

SERVES
4+2

This is the faster way to a fun food.

PREPARATION TIME
15 MINUTES

1 tsp (5 mL) canola oil
8 spinach lasagna noodles
2 tsp (10 mL) olive oil

1 pkg (8 oz/225 g) Veggie
   Ground Round
1 can (19 oz/540 mL) tomato
   sauce

8 oz (250 g) shredded
   mozzarella cheese
2 tsp (10 mL) dried oregano
   or basil (optional)

Tips

Veggie Ground Round is a great
ingredient not just for its nutritional value but also for its ease of
use. It needs no browning before
adding so can be tossed into
many recipes at any point. Should
you have excess or extra packages of it, try sprinkling it on pizza.
It will look like ground beef and
add protein to this family staple.

• Bring large pot of water to boil; add canola oil. Immerse lasagna noodles in water; boil until
just softened but not sticky, 10 to 12 minutes. Drain and lay out flat on clean counter or
plastic wrap.

• Meanwhile, oil large lasagna pan with olive oil and set aside. In large bowl, mix ground round
with tomato sauce. Spread some onto each lasagna noodle; top with small amount of
cheese. Roll up and place in oiled pan. Top with more sauce and cheese. Sprinkle with
oregano if desired. (Cover and refrigerate up to 2 days.) Bake in 350°F (180°C) oven for
20 minutes. (Let cool, cover and refrigerate up to 2 days.)

Boston Baked Beans

Serve with a few low-fat corn chips, some slices of avocado and celery sticks for a "cowboy supper."

4 slices bacon
2 cups (500 mL) chopped
   onion
1 lb (500 g) dried navy beans
   (2 cups/500 mL)

8 cups (2 L) water
1/2 cup (125 mL) fancy
   molasses (approx)
2 tbsp (30 mL) brown mustard
Salt and pepper to taste

1 tsp (5 mL) cider vinegar
   (approx)

- Using large heavy pot with tight-fitting lid, cook bacon over medium heat for about 7 minutes until browned and fat is released. Add onion; cook, stirring often, for about 8 minutes.
- Meanwhile, rinse beans in colander; remove any discoloured beans or pebbles. Add to pot along with water, molasses, mustard, salt and pepper. Bring to boil and stir for about 10 minutes. Cover and bake in bottom third of 300°F (150°C) oven for 6 hours until softened. (Or cook in slow-cooker at high for 6 to 8 hours.) Uncover and bake for 1 1/2 hours longer or until sauce thickens, stirring occasionally. If desired, stir in an extra teaspoon (5 mL) each of molasses and vinegar to balance flavours. (Freeze in small serving sizes.)

Tips

Have children rinse beans in a colander and look for any small rocks or pebbles. Anyone who finds one wins a taste of sweet molasses right off of the spoon.

This recipe is a hit for kids when they find out that they are guaranteed to be musical within a few hours of eating. Boys especially find these things funny.

Homemade Chicken Fingers

SERVES
8

PREPARATION TIME
14 MINUTES

If chicken tenders are available at your grocery store, buy them. They eliminate the need for slicing the breast and are also the softer texture that most kids prefer.

These fingers use a fraction of the fat and salt of store-bought chicken fingers. Since they are baked rather than deep-fried, there is no trans fat. The addition of cornmeal gives the fingers some crunch but also adds fibre and an extra grain to the diet.

Serve with carrot and celery sticks, and with salsa as a dip to get extra veggies in. This bread crumb mixture is sufficient to coat 8 lb (3.5 kg) of chicken, but we are only preparing 2 lb (1 kg), so the extra can be stored for future use.

4 cups (1 L) dry whole wheat
bread crumbs
1 cup (250 mL) cornmeal
1 tbsp (15 mL) paprika
2 tsp (10 mL) celery salt

2 tsp (10 mL) onion salt
2 tsp (10 mL) poultry
seasoning
1 tsp (5 mL) white pepper
1 tsp (5 mL) dried basil

1/2 tsp (2 mL) garlic powder
1/2 cup (125 mL) canola oil
2 lb (1 kg) boneless skinless
chicken breasts

• In large bowl, stir together bread crumbs, cornmeal, paprika, celery salt, onion salt, poultry seasoning, pepper, basil and garlic powder. Add oil and mix again. Divide into 4 large resealable plastic bags; freeze 3 for up to 3 months. Use one for this recipe.

• Pat chicken dry with paper towels. Cut each breast lengthwise into 3 or 4 strips. Add strips, 2 at a time, to one of the bags; shake until evenly coated. Lay on baking sheet sprayed with vegetable oil spray. (Freeze until solid; transfer to freezer bags and freeze for up to 3 weeks. Bake, frozen, in 325°F/160°C oven for 20 to 30 minutes.)

• Bake in 350°F (180°C) oven for 10 to 15 minutes or until no longer pink inside.

Cucumber Faces

This is an afterschool snack as well as an art activity—how can you go wrong?

2 English cucumbers	**2 carrots**	**1/2 cup (125 mL) light cream cheese**

- Slice cucumbers into rounds. Grate carrots into bowl.
- Spread cream cheese onto cucumber rounds. Allow each child to make as many funny faces as they can by sticking on strips of carrot for eyes, nose and mouth. Cover and refrigerate.

**SERVES
8**

**PREPARATION TIME
2 MINUTES**

Tip

Most kids will eat cucumbers although they are not the most nutritious vegetable. So we start showing our commitment to vegetables by making this one fun. We use English cucumbers because their skins are thin enough to be washed and eaten. The waxy kind are not good for this and provide even fewer vitamins.

Bonus Kids Week Shopping List

YOU NEED:

Light cream cheese (1/2 cup/125 mL)
Shredded mozzarella cheese
  (8 oz/250 g)
Bacon (4 slices)
Boneless skinless chicken breasts
  (2 lb/1 kg)
Veggie Ground Round (1 pkg, 8 oz/225 g)
Onions (2)
English cucumbers (2)
*Avocados (2)
*Celery (1 head)
Carrots (2)
*Low-fat corn chips (1 pkg)

CHECK YOUR PANTRY FOR:

Whole wheat bread crumbs (4 cups/1 L)
Brown mustard (2 tbsp/30 mL)
Canola oil (1/2 cup + 1 tsp/130 mL)
Olive oil (2 tsp/10 mL)
Molasses (1/2 cup/125 mL)
Dried navy beans (1 lb/500 g)
Cornmeal (1 cup/250 mL)
Spinach lasagna noodles (1 lb/500 g)
Poultry seasoning (2 tsp/10 mL)
Dried basil (1 tsp/5 mL)
Dried oregano (2 tsp/10 mL)
White pepper (1 tsp/5 mL)
Garlic powder (1 tsp/5 mL)
Celery salt (2 tsp/10 mL)
Paprika (1 tbsp/15 mL)
Onion salt (2 tsp/10 mL)
Tomato sauce (1 can, 19 oz/540 mL)
Cider vinegar (1 tsp/5 mL)
Salsa (1 jar)

*grab and go items

Notes

I believe that every mouthful should have some nutritional value, but this doesn't mean we can't have a treat now and then. All of the desserts here have at least one thing going for them: they might contain a fruit or a vegetable, protein in the form of nuts, whole grains or perhaps a little of each. You will not find one drop of trans fat. You will find only real butter, whole eggs and a bit of sugar.

Many of these desserts and snacks are just fine to be served as breakfast. Sugary cereals contain minimal amounts of protein, minerals and vitamins for their calories, but our desserts, containing good things like sweet potatoes, pumpkin and zucchini, are nutritionally dense in comparison. Best of all, they're fun to eat and easy to make.

Desserts and Snacks

Crisp Topping

Pumpkin Pie

Sweet Potato Muffins

Zucchini Muffins

Oh Mega Crackers

Oatmeal Cookies

Quick and Delicious Peanut Butter Cookies

Whole Wheat Graham Crackers

Chewy Biscotti

Banana Boats

Granola Bars

Q-Bix

Sticky Rice Pudding

Vanilla Almond Shake

Crisp Topping

SERVES
12

PREPARATION TIME
10 MINUTES

Tip

Choose any frozen fruit you desire; we like apples or blueberries. Microwave a bowl of frozen fruit until melted and warmed. Top with a spoonful or two of the topping. A dollop of low-fat vanilla yogurt makes it even better. You can also use this to top ice cream or sliced berries. A little goes a long way.

Yes, there is butter and sugar in this topping but there are also oats and almonds, so the key will be portion size. Kids can eat this by the handful like a granola but the best way to serve it is with warm fruit (see Tip).

1/4 cup (50 mL) whole wheat flour
1 cup (250 mL) packed brown sugar

1 cup (250 mL) rolled oats
1 cup (250 mL) slivered almonds
1 tsp (5 mL) cinnamon

1/4 tsp (1 mL) nutmeg
1/2 cup (125 mL) butter, melted

• In bowl, combine flour, sugar, oats, nuts, cinnamon and nutmeg; blend in butter until crumbly. Spread on baking sheet. Bake in top third of 375°F (190°C) oven for 18 to 20 minutes until browned and crispy. Let cool completely. Refrigerate in jar or resealable plastic bag for up to 3 weeks.

Pumpkin Pie

SERVES
6

PREPARATION TIME
10 MINUTES

It is the crust that makes pumpkin pie so decadent, but the truth is that pumpkin is a very nutritious vegetable. If we can garner all of the good and dispense with the bad, we can serve dessert every night!

1 can (28 oz/796 mL) pumpkin	2 eggs	2 tbsp (30 mL) pumpkin pie
3/4 cup (175 mL) evaporated	1/2 (125 mL) cup packed	spice
skim milk	brown sugar	1/4 tsp (1 mL) cream of tartar

• Butter and flour pie plate; set aside. In bowl, mix together pumpkin, evaporated milk, eggs, sugar, pumpkin pie spice and cream of tartar; pour into prepared pie plate. Bake in 350°F (180°C) oven for 1 hour or until firm.

Sweet Potato Muffins

SERVES
12

PREPARATION TIME
30 MINUTES

If you have leftover sweet potatoes, they are the best to use. If not, microwave two medium sweet potatoes, peel and then mash them.

Freeze in single wrappers for lunches or snacks. Serve for dessert or warm in oven for breakfast.

1/2 cup (125 mL) butter,
  softened
1 cup (250 mL) packed brown
  sugar
1 1/2 cups (375 mL) mashed
  cooked sweet potatoes

1 egg
3/4 cup (175 mL) whole
  wheat flour
3/4 cup (175 mL) all-purpose
  flour

2 tsp (10 mL) pumpkin pie
  spice
1 tsp (5 mL) baking soda
1/3 cup (75 mL) milk (approx)

- In bowl and using electric mixer, cream butter and brown sugar together until fluffy. Beat in sweet potatoes and egg.
- Sift together whole wheat and all-purpose flours, pumpkin pie spice and baking soda. Mix half into sweet potato mixture. Add only enough milk to thin batter. Add remaining dry ingredients. Add enough of the milk to make very thick batter.
- Butter and flour muffin pan or use muffin papers. Fill muffin cups two-thirds full. Bake in 375°F (190°C) oven until dry on top and fork comes out clean, 15 to 22 minutes. Let cool. Wrap individually and freeze.

Zucchini Muffins

SERVES
24

PREPARATION TIME
30 MINUTES

When your neighbour's garden overgrows huge zucchini onto your side of the fence, you now have a solution.

3 eggs	1 1/2 cups (375 mL) all-purpose flour	1 tsp (5 mL) nutmeg
1 2/3 cups (400 mL) granulated sugar	1 1/2 cups (375 mL) whole wheat flour	3 cups (750 mL) coarsely shredded zucchini
1/2 cup (125 mL) canola oil	2 tsp (10 mL) cinnamon	1 cup (250 mL) seedless raisins (optional)
1/4 cup (50 mL) butter, softened	1 tsp (5 mL) baking powder	2 tbsp (30 mL) ground flaxseed
1/4 cup (50 mL) almond butter	1 tsp (5 mL) baking soda	
1 1/2 tsp (7 mL) vanilla	1 tsp (5 mL) salt	

- In bowl, beat eggs until light with hand whisk or electric beaters. Gradually add sugar, oil, butter then almond butter and vanilla.

- In separate bowl and using fork, mix together all-purpose and whole wheat flours, cinnamon, baking powder, baking soda, salt and nutmeg. Add zucchini. Add to sugar mixture and beat until smooth. Stir in raisins if desired and flaxseed.

- Spoon into non-stick muffin cups until three-quarters full. Bake in 350°F (180°C) oven 12 to 15 minutes for mini muffins, 15 to 20 for full size. Let cool. Freeze and warm for 15 seconds in microwave oven.

Oh Mega Crackers

MAKES
18

SERVES
18

PREPARATION TIME
15 MINUTES

These are named for their high omega-3 content derived from nuts and wheat germ.

3 tbsp (45 mL) wheat germ
1 tsp (5 mL) packed brown
 sugar
1 tsp (5 mL) dry yeast
1/3 cup (75 mL) warm water
 (105° to 115°F/40° to 46°C)
1/4 cup (50 mL) ground
 almonds

1 tbsp (15 mL) ground
 flaxseed
1 tbsp (15 mL) olive oil
1 tsp (5 mL) salt
3/4 cup (175 mL) whole
 wheat flour

2 to 3 tbsp (30 to 45 mL)
 all-purpose flour for
 rolling out
1 tsp (5 mL) onion salt
1 tsp (5 mL) garlic powder
1 tsp (5 mL) chili powder

- Spread wheat germ on baking sheet; bake in 350°F (180°C) oven for 10 minutes, stirring after 5 minutes. Set aside.
- In large bowl, dissolve brown sugar and yeast in warm water; let stand 5 minutes. Add wheat germ, almonds, flaxseed, oil and salt; stir well. Stir in whole wheat flour to form stiff dough. Turn out onto lightly floured surface. Knead until smooth and elastic, about 10 minutes, adding only enough all-purpose flour, 1 tbsp (15 mL) at a time, to prevent dough from sticking to hands. Place in bowl coated with cooking spray, turning to coat top. Cover and let rise in warm (85°F/29°C) draft-free place until doubled in bulk.
- Punch dough down, Roll into 10-1/2 x 9-inch (26 x 23 cm) paper-thin rectangle on baking sheet coated with cooking spray. Score by making lengthwise and crosswise cuts to form 18 crackers. Prick surface liberally with fork. Sprinkle with onion salt, garlic powder and chili powder.
- Bake in 350°F (180°C) oven for 15 minutes or until browned and crisp. Remove from pan; let cool completely on wire rack. Separate into crackers and store in airtight container.

Oatmeal Cookies

Keep a close eye on these cookies as you bake: 8 to 10 minutes will make them soft but 10 to 12 will make them crispy. If you want chewier cookies, leave dough in a ball, which will flatten during baking. If you like them crispy then press slightly flat before you bake.

MAKES
60

SERVES
30

PREPARATION TIME
15 MINUTES

1 cup (250 mL) butter
2 cups (500 mL) all-purpose
  flour
1 tsp (5 mL) cinnamon
1 tsp (5 mL) baking soda

1 tsp (5 mL) baking powder
1 cup (250 mL) packed brown
  sugar
1 cup (250 mL) granulated
  sugar

2 eggs, beaten lightly
3 cups (750 mL) rolled oats
1/2 cup (125 mL) seedless
  raisins

• Melt butter and cool to room temperature; place in large bowl. In separate bowl, sift together flour, cinnamon, baking soda and baking powder. Add brown and granulated sugars to butter and stir well. Add eggs, sifted dry ingredients, oats and raisins. Drop by spoonfuls onto well-greased baking sheets. Bake in 350°F (180°C) oven for 10 minutes.

Quick and Delicious Peanut Butter Cookies

MAKES
24

SERVES
12

PREPARATION TIME
30 MINUTES

You can feel okay about serving these for breakfast. They are a good source of protein served with a glass of milk.

1 cup (250 mL) peanut butter (natural, unsweetened without hydrogenated oils)	**2/3 cup (150 mL) granulated sugar**	**1 tsp (5 mL) all-purpose flour**
	1 egg	

- In bowl, combine peanut butter, sugar and egg; blend well. Sprinkle with flour to make balls easier to shape.
- Form into 24 1-inch (2.5 cm) balls. Place 1 1/2 to 2 inches (4 to 5 cm) apart on greased baking sheets. Using fork, press crisscross pattern into dough.
- Bake in 350°F (180°C) oven 12 to 15 minutes or until lightly browned. Cool on wire rack.

Whole Wheat Graham Crackers

MAKES
12–18

SERVES
6

If you wish to double the batch, you have two options: bake and then freeze until ready for use or freeze dough and thaw at room temperature for 2 to 4 hours and roll out as directed for a fresher product.

PREPARATION TIME
15 MINUTES

2 cups (500 mL) whole wheat flour
3/4 cup (175 mL) butter

1 tsp (5 mL) baking soda
1 tsp (5 mL) cream of tartar
1/3 cup (75 mL) frozen apple juice concentrate, thawed

1 egg
2 tbsp (30 mL) hot water

- Place flour in large bowl. Cut in butter until it looks like little peas. Add baking soda, cream of tartar, apple juice concentrate, egg and just enough water to make dough that can be rolled thin.
- Flour counter and roll out dough as thinly as possible. Cut into 4-inch (10 cm) squares with pizza wheel. Bake on baking sheet lined with parchment paper or foil in 350°F (180°C) oven for 15 minutes or until starting to brown at edges, watching carefully to remove end crackers as they brown if centre ones are still soft.
- Pull parchment paper off baking sheet and let crackers cool completely. Store in airtight container up to 2 weeks. Place sheet of paper towel in container to absorb any moisture that may make these crackers soft.

Chewy Biscotti

MAKES
12

SERVES
12

PREPARATION TIME
20 MINUTES

You have a choice here on whether to serve these soft like a cake or crunchy like a cookie. As a cake, just leave as is but if you want a more portable "biscotti," then lay out on baking sheet and bake in a 325°F (160°C) oven for 15 minutes until crisp.

1 1/4 cups (300 mL) dates, finely chopped
1 cup (250 mL) frozen apple juice concentrate, thawed

1/4 cup (50 mL) canola oil
2 egg whites
1 tsp (5 mL) vanilla
1 cup (250 mL) whole wheat flour

1/2 cup (125 mL) wheat germ
1 1/2 tsp (7 mL) baking powder
2 tsp (10 mL) cinnamon

Tip

As a special treat, dip these in melted chocolate. Simply melt 4 oz (125 g) bittersweet chocolate over a double boiler and stir in 2 tbsp (30 mL) butter. Dip one end of the biscotti into the warm chocolate and then place on a baking sheet covered with foil. Allow to cool and peel off. Great for a holiday buffet or teacher's gift.

• In saucepan, bring dates and apple juice concentrate to boil. Remove from heat and let cool for 10 minutes. Stir in oil and let cool to room temperature, at least 1 hour. (You can speed this up by placing in fridge.)

• In metal bowl, beat egg whites until slightly frothy; stir into date mixture. Stir in vanilla. In mixing bowl, combine flour, wheat germ, baking powder and cinnamon; stir in date mixture just until combined.

• Rub loaf pan with butter; pour in batter. Bake in 350°F (180°C) oven 45 to 50 minutes until toothpick comes out clean. Let cool slightly before removing from pan to wire rack. Let cool completely; slice into 12 sticks.

Banana Boats

SERVES
4

Top with vanilla ice cream or lemon sorbet for special occasions.

PREPARATION TIME
5 MINUTES

4 bananas	**2 tbsp (30 mL) carob or chocolate chips**	**2 tbsp (30 mL) miniature marshmallows**

- Slit bananas lengthwise but not all the way through. Sprinkle carob chips and marshmallows evenly in each banana cavity. Wrap well in foil.
- Bake in 450°F (230°C) oven or toaster oven or on barbecue for 15 to 20 minutes until marshmallows and chips are melted.

Granola Bars

MAKES
12

SERVES
12

PREPARATION TIME
20 MINUTES

These are a great after school snack filled with complex carbs and protein. The addition of raisins and/or chocolate chips makes an easier sell.

1 cup (250 mL) rolled oats
1 cup (250 mL) slivered
  almonds
2/3 cup (150 mL) packed
  brown sugar

2/3 cup (150 mL) raisins
  (optional)
1/4 cup (50 mL) whole wheat
  flour
1/4 cup (50 mL) chocolate
  chips (optional)

1 tbsp (15 mL) brewer's yeast
2 tsp (10 mL) cinnamon
1/2 tsp (2 mL) nutmeg
1/2 cup (125 mL) butter

- In bowl, stir together rolled oats, almonds, brown sugar, raisins if desired, flour, chocolate chips if desired, brewer's yeast, cinnamon and nutmeg. Melt butter in microwave oven for 30 to 45 seconds; stir into mixture.

- Firmly press mixture onto foil-lined baking sheet. (It will fill pan only halfway so scrunch up remaining foil to hold mixture in place.) Bake on top rack of 375°F (190°C) oven for about 20 minutes until browned and bubbling. Let cool for 2 to 4 minutes or until sound of bubbling stops. Cut into squares or bars while still hot. Store in airtight container for up to 3 weeks.

Q-Bix

This no-bake snack does not travel well but is great for breakfast. A glass of milk and a couple Q-bix is all you need to send children off for the day with enough protein, dairy and whole grain carbs to get them to lunch.

1/2 cup (125 mL) almond butter
1/3 cup (75 mL) rolled oats
1/4 cup (50 mL) dry milk powder

1/4 cup (50 mL) shredded coconut
1/4 cup (50 mL) wheat germ
1/4 cup (50 mL) frozen apple juice concentrate, thawed

2 tbsp (30 mL) raisins (optional)
1/2 tsp (2 mL) cinnamon
1/4 cup (50 mL) cocoa powder (optional)

MAKES
16

SERVES
8

PREPARATION TIME
15 MINUTES

- In large bowl, thoroughly combine almond butter, rolled oats, milk powder, coconut, wheat germ, apple juice, raisins if desired and cinnamon. Shape into 16 1-inch (2.5 cm) cubes. Measure cocoa powder into bowl and drop cubes in one at a time to coat.
- Place on baking sheet or baking pan and chill thoroughly before serving, at least 1 hour. Store in airtight container in refrigerator.

Sticky Rice Pudding

SERVES
16

PREPARATION TIME
10 MINUTES

Search until you find a short-grain brown rice. Try the health food section at the grocery store, the health-food store or Asian markets.

**1 1/2 cups (375 mL) short-
grain brown rice
3 cups (750 mL) water**

**2 cups (500 mL) milk
1 cup (250 mL) golden raisins
1 cup (250 mL) liquid honey**

**2 tbsp (30 mL) cinnamon
(approx)**

• In very large pot, mix rice with water; bring to boil. Reduce heat and simmer for 45 to 55 minutes until rice is tender. Turn off heat. Add milk, raisins, honey and cinnamon; let stand for 15 to 30 minutes to absorb milk. Serve warm with sprinkle of cinnamon.

Vanilla Almond Shake

Really quite tasty, this shake is loaded with "good fats" and calories that will make up for any skipped meal.

2 cups (500 mL) vanilla soy
  milk
1/2 cup (125 mL) silken tofu

1/4 cup (50 mL) ice cubes
1 tbsp (15 mL) almond butter
1 ripe banana

1 tbsp (15 mL) ground
  flaxseed

SERVES
2

PREPARATION TIME
3 MINUTES

• In blender, blend together soy milk, tofu, ice, almond butter, banana and flaxseed.

Nutritional Analysis

Analyses are per serving. Each recipe has been divided by the total number of servings, including both supper and leftover portions. In recipes calling for stock, I have provided analyses using a 1 to 1 mixture of canned stock and water. The sodium levels in these analyses are very high. Choosing homemade or frozen stock provides a much lower sodium count.

Asian Sprout and Red Pepper Salad: Calories 80, Fat 7 g, Carbohydrates 4 g, Fibre 1 g, Protein 2 g, Sodium 33 mg

Asparagus in Its Own Juices: Calories 77, Fat 6 g, Carbohydrates 6 g, Fibre 2 g, Protein 2 g, Sodium 270 mg

Athenian Lamb and Lima Beans: Calories 329, Fat 10 g, Carbohydrates 38 g, Fibre 7 g, Protein 26 g, Sodium 760 mg

Baked Mashed Potatoes and Potato Skins: Calories 233, Fat 8 g, Carbohydrates 36 g, Fibre 5 g, Protein 6 g, Sodium 202 mg

Baked Pork Tenderloin with Spinach and Blue Cheese: Calories 344, Fat 14 g, Carbohydrates 11 g, Fibre 5 g, Protein 43 g, Sodium 595 mg

Balsamic Barley Salad: Calories 256, Fat 7 g, Carbohydrates 42 g, Fibre 8 g, Protein 10 g, Sodium 405 mg

Banana Boats: Calories 143, Fat 3 g, Carbohydrates 32 g, Fibre 3 g, Protein 2 g, Sodium 3 mg

Barley Risotto (using canned stock and water): Calories 208, Fat 3 g, Carbohydrates 35 g, Fibre 7 g, Protein 9 g, Sodium 1733 mg

Beef Tenderloin Steaks with Peppercorn Rub: Calories 423, Fat 29 g, Carbohydrates 15 g, Fibre 3 g, Protein 26 g, Sodium 677 mg

Better Spaghetti Sauce: Calories 279, Fat 13 g, Carbohydrates 19 g, Fibre 5 g, Protein 14 g, Sodium 605 mg

Bistro Burgers: Calories 405, Fat 21 g, Carbohydrates 17 g, Fibre 4 g, Protein 27 g, Sodium 397 mg

Black Bean Nachos: Calories 592, Fat 20 g, Carbohydrates 78 g, Fibre 18 g, Protein 31 g, Sodium 626 mg

Boston Baked Beans: Calories 282, Fat 3 g, Carbohydrates 52 g, Fibre 15 g, Protein 14 g, Sodium 125 mg

Celery Peanut Butter Logs: Calories 190, Fat 16 g, Carbohydrates 7 g, Fibre 2 g, Protein 8 g, Sodium 159 mg

Chewy Biscotti: Calories 186, Fat 5 g, Carbohydrates 34 g, Fibre 4 g, Protein 4 g, Sodium 55 mg

Chicken Breasts with Spicy Rub: Calories 424, Fat 24 g, Carbohydrates 13 g, Fibre 1 g, Protein 39 g, Sodium 705 mg

Chicken Cacciatore: Calories 312, Fat 12 g, Carbohydrates 19 g, Fibre 9 g, Protein 39 g, Sodium 1242 mg

Chicken Soup (using canned stock and water): Calories 136, Fat 1 g, Carbohydrates 15 g, Fibre 3 g, Protein 14 g, Sodium 2223 mg

Chicken Stuffed with Sun-Dried Tomatoes and Chèvre: Calories 372, Fat 11 g, Carbohydrates 39 g, Fibre 8 g, Protein 37 g, Sodium 1548 mg

Creamy Baked Salmon: Calories 177, Fat 4 g, Carbohydrates 7 g, Fibre 0 g, Protein 27 g, Sodium 275 mg

Crisp Topping: Calories 227, Fat 13 g, Carbohydrates 26 g, Fibre 2 g, Protein 4 g, Sodium 86 mg

Crustless Broccoli and Cheese Quiches: Calories 390, Fat 29 g, Carbohydrates 14 g, Fibre 1 g, Protein 19 g, Sodium 438 mg

Cucumber Faces: Calories 60, Fat 3 g, Carbohydrates 7 g, Fibre 2 g, Protein 3 g, Sodium 89 mg

Easy Minestrone: Calories 271, Fat 8 g, Carbohydrates 41 g, Fibre 10 g, Protein 12 g, Sodium 918 mg

Five-Spice Chicken with Hot Slaw: Calories 379, Fat 10 g, Carbohydrates 23 g, Fibre 3 g, Protein 50 g, Sodium 1427 mg

Granola Bars: Calories 254, Fat 15 g, Carbohydrates 30 g, Fibre 3 g, Protein 4 g, Sodium 86 mg

Grilled Vegetable Soup (using canned stock and water): Calories 383, Fat 23 g, Carbohydrates 23 g, Fibre 4 g, Protein 21 g, Sodium 3179 mg

Guacamole: Calories 177, Fat 16 g, Carbohydrates 11 g, Fibre 4 g, Protein 3 g, Sodium 26 mg

Homemade Chicken Fingers: Calories 233, Fat 6 g, Carbohydrates 14 g, Fibre 1 g, Protein 28 g, Sodium 393 mg

Jamaican-ish Pork: Calories 183, Fat 6 g, Carbohydrates 2 g, Fibre 1 g, Protein 29 g, Sodium 240 mg

Lasagna Roll-Ups: Calories 645, Fat 13 g, Carbohydrates 98 g, Fibre 7 g, Protein 34 g, Sodium 978 mg

Lemony Baked Shrimp: Calories 372, Fat 10 g, Carbohydrates 20 g, Fibre 1 g, Protein 49 g, Sodium 779 mg

Lower-Fat Chili Con Carne: Calories 423, Fat 13 g, Carbohydrates 55 g, Fibre 21 g, Protein 26 g, Sodium 381 mg

Meat Loaf Florentine with Salsa: Calories 391, Fat 24 g, Carbohydrates 18 g, Fibre 3 g, Protein 26 g, Sodium 811 mg

Molasses Lentil Soup (using canned stock and water): Calories 359, Fat 5 g, Carbohydrates 52 g, Fibre 18 g, Protein 27 g, Sodium 2203 mg

Oatmeal Cookies: Calories 181, Fat 7 g, Carbohydrates 28 g, Fibre 1 g, Protein 3 g, Sodium 128 mg

Oh Mega Crackers: Calories 48, Fat 2 g, Carbohydrates 6 g, Fibre 1 g, Protein 2 g, Sodium 190 mg

Parsnip Purée Chicken Stew (using canned stock and water): Calories 360, Fat 11 g, Carbohydrates 42 g, Fibre 9 g, Protein 24 g, Sodium 973 mg

Poppy Seed Noodles: Calories 118, Fat 5 g, Carbohydrates 15 g, Fibre 1 g, Protein 3 g, Sodium 5 mg

Pork Roast Dijon: Calories 599, Fat 29 g, Carbohydrates 36 g, Fibre 5 g, Protein 40 g, Sodium 263 mg

Pumpkin Pie: Calories 128, Fat 2 g, Carbohydrates 25 g, Fibre 3 g, Protein 5 g, Sodium 54 mg

Q-Bix: Calories 181, Fat 12 g, Carbohydrates 16 g, Fibre 3 g, Protein 6 g, Sodium 21 mg

Quick and Delicious Peanut Butter Cookies: Calories 177, Fat 11 g, Carbohydrates 16 g, Fibre 1 g, Protein 6 g, Sodium 108 mg

Quick Italian Sausage and Kidney Bean Soup (using canned stock and water): Calories 271, Fat 6 g, Carbohydrates 41 g, Fibre 13 g, Protein 13 g, Sodium 2215 mg

Quinoa and Carrots (made with water): Calories 209, Fat 5 g, Carbohydrates 35 g, Fibre 5 g, Protein 6 g, Sodium 79 mg

Red Pepper Rice: Calories 181, Fat 2 g, Carbohydrates 37 g, Fibre 1 g, Protein 4 g, Sodium 367 mg

Rice with Grated Carrots (using canned stock and water): Calories 197, Fat 2 g, Carbohydrates 39 g, Fibre 2 g, Protein 4 g, Sodium 1087 mg

Roast Beef with Rosemary and Garlic Veggies: Calories 220, Fat 9 g, Carbohydrates 6 g, Fibre 1 g, Protein 26 g, Sodium 333 mg

Roasted Chicken to Please Everybody (with skin): Calories 560, Fat 31 g, Carbohydrates 30 g, Fibre 4 g, Protein 36 g, Sodium 386 mg

Roasted Vegetables with Garlic Oil: Calories 131, Fat 5 g, Carbohydrates 20 g, Fibre 5 g, Protein 4 g, Sodium 150 mg

Salmon Cakes with Caper Mayo: Calories 365, Fat 15 g, Carbohydrates 29 g, Fibre 2 g, Protein 28 g, Sodium 837 mg

Salmon with Spinach and Feta in Parchment: Calories 325, Fat 17 g, Carbohydrates 12 g, Fibre 5 g, Protein 36 g, Sodium 815 mg

Scallops and Soy Beans in Sake Stock (using canned stock and water): Calories 372, Fat 13 g, Carbohydrates 10 g, Fibre 6 g, Protein 32 g, Sodium 980 mg

Sesame Broccoli Salad: Calories 68, Fat 6 g, Carbohydrates 3 g, Fibre 1 g, Protein 2 g, Sodium 307 mg

Sesame Fish Cakes with Baby Bok Choy: Calories 400, Fat 3 g, Carbohydrates 56 g, Fibre 6 g, Protein 39 g, Sodium 2542 mg

Slow-Cooked Beer-Braised Beef: Calories 541, Fat 36 g, Carbohydrates 9 g, Fibre 1 g, Protein 37 g, Sodium 207 mg

Southwestern Fish Sticks: Calories 253, Fat 4 g, Carbohydrates 27 g, Fibre 2 g, Protein 27 g, Sodium 500 mg

Souvlaki Pork with Tossed Greek Salad: Calories 275, Fat 15 g, Carbohydrates 8 g, Fibre 1 g, Protein 28 g, Sodium 234 mg

Spicy Coconut Salad: Calories 107, Fat 6 g, Carbohydrates 14 g, Fibre 2 g, Protein 3 g, Sodium 16 mg

Steamed Broccoli: Calories 9, Fat 0 g, Carbohydrates 1 g, Fibre 1 g, Protein 1 g, Sodium 51 mg

Steamed Dilly Carrots: Calories 52, Fat 1 g, Carbohydrates 12 g, Fibre 3 g, Protein 1 g, Sodium 573 mg

Steamed Snow Peas: Calories 27, Fat 0 g, Carbohydrates 5 g, Fibre 1 g, Protein 1 g, Sodium 2 mg

Sticky Rice Pudding: Calories 181, Fat 2 g, Carbohydrates 41 g, Fibre 1 g, Protein 3 g, Sodium 19 mg

Sunday Ham with Potatoes: Calories 520, Fat 31 g, Carbohydrates 23 g, Fibre 2 g, Protein 38 g, Sodium 231 mg

Sunday Ham Soup with Romano Beans and Kale: Calories 155, Fat 5 g, Carbohydrates 18 g, Fibre 3 g, Protein 10 g, Sodium 532 mg

Sweet Potato Muffins: Calories 219, Fat 9 g, Carbohydrates 34 g, Fibre 2 g, Protein 3 g, Sodium 201 mg

Thai Stuffed Pork with Mashed Apples and Squash: Calories 427, Fat 14 g, Carbohydrates 30 g, Fibre 3 g, Protein 43 g, Sodium 170 mg

Tofu Caesar Salad: Calories 39, Fat 3 g, Carbohydrates 2 g, Fibre 1 g, Protein 3 g, Sodium 30 mg

Tuna Sailboats: Calories 282, Fat 12 g, Carbohydrates 31 g, Fibre 5 g, Protein 16 g, Sodium 503 mg

Vanilla Almond Shake: Calories 302, Fat 18 g, Carbohydrates 26 g, Fibre 8 g, Protein 16 g, Sodium 45 mg

Veggies week 2: Calories 58, Fat 0 g, Carbohydrates 12 g, Fibre 4 g, Protein 3 g, Sodium 19 mg

Veggies week 4: Calories 124, Fat 1 g, Carbohydrates 29 g, Fibre 9 g, Protein 4 g, Sodium 88 mg

Whole Wheat Graham Crackers: Calories 309, Fat 17 g, Carbohydrates 36 g, Fibre 5 g, Protein 7 g, Sodium 381 mg

Zucchini Muffins: Calories 221, Fat 9 g, Carbohydrates 32 g, Fibre 2 g, Protein 4 g, Sodium 192 mg

As analyzed with Sierra MasterCook program and rounded to the nearest whole number.

Make-Ahead Mixes and Salad Dressings

We have come to rely on packaged mixes to make our weeknight suppers faster, but nothing could be simpler to do at home with healthier, fresher, less-expensive ingredients. Our homemade Cheese Coating is great to use for chicken fingers, or for baked vegetables or potatoes. Salad dressings, too, can be made better and less expensively at home. Here are some mix and dressing ideas that can be made ahead and stored in the fridge or cupboard. Kids love to mix these ingredients and my cooking class kids have invented variations that have surprised and delighted all of us.

Chili Spice

Use this mix by the teaspoonful to spice up any dish that is bland enough for the kids but needs a little zip for more grown-up tastebuds. It is great in tomato sauce or in our biscuit mix.

1/2 cup (125 mL) chili powder	8 tsp (40 mL) ground cumin	2 tsp (10 mL) garlic powder
1/4 cup (50 mL) Mrs. Dash seasoning	4 tsp (20 mL) dried oregano	1 tsp (5 mL) cayenne pepper
	4 tsp (20 mL) onion powder	

• Mix together chili powder, Mrs. Dash, cumin, oregano, onion powder, garlic powder and cayenne. Store in airtight container for up to 3 months.

Cheese Coating

Use to coat chicken, zucchini cubes or chopped sweet potatoes.

4 cups (1 L) dry whole wheat breadcrumbs	3/4 cup (175 mL) grated Parmesan cheese	1 tsp (5 mL) garlic powder
1 cup (250 mL) dried parsley	1/2 cup (125 mL) olive oil	1 tsp (5 mL) salt
		1 tsp (5 mL) pepper

• Mix together bread crumbs, parsley, cheese, oil, garlic powder, salt and pepper. Refrigerate in airtight container for up to 4 weeeks or freeze up to 8 weeks. Coat chosen food in mixture; lay on baking sheet. Bake in 400°F (200°C) oven until cooked through. (Veggies need 10 to15 minutes; chicken may need 40.)

Whole Wheat Biscuit Mix

Great for last-minute biscuits to go with any meal!

4 cups (1 L) whole wheat flour
2 cups (500 mL) unbleached flour
1 1/2 cups (375 mL) skim milk powder

1 cup (250 mL) granulated sugar
3/4 cup (175 mL) wheat germ
1/2 cup (125 mL) plus 2 tbsp (30 mL) baking powder

1 tbsp (15 mL) salt
1 1/2 cups (375 mL) butter

• In bowl, mix together whole wheat and unbleached flours, milk powder, sugar, wheat germ, baking powder and salt; cut in butter. Store in fridge up to 3 weeks.

• Stir 2 cups (500 mL) of mix with one egg and mix in just enough water to make sticky dough. Drop by rounded spoonfuls onto baking sheet; bake for 10 to 25 minutes in 375°F (190°C) oven. Makes about 60 biscuits.

VARIATIONS:

• Add different liquids such as apple juice or buttermilk instead of water.

• Stir in some Chili Spice and cornmeal to make cornmeal muffins.

• Stir in extra milk and one egg and use as a pancake mix; be sure to thin it out considerably.

• Add a handful of rolled oats and a mashed banana and bake as muffins in muffin tins.

Sesame Topping

Use to add a crunchy twist to any meal. Sprinkle into a salad and use our Asian Dressing. Top any stir-fry to add some crunch and fibre. Sprinkle into soups instead of crackers. Serve as is for a great snack alternative to chips or popcorn.

2 cups (500 mL) rolled oats
1/2 cup (125 mL) melted butter

1/3 cup (75 mL) shredded extra-old Cheddar cheese

1/3 cup (75 mL) sesame seeds
1/4 cup (50 mL) garlic powder

• In bowl, combine oats, butter, cheese, sesame seeds and garlic powder; spread on baking sheet. Bake in 350°F (180°C) oven for 15 minutes or until lightly browned. Store in refrigerator up to 2 months.

Asian Dressing

1/2 cup (125 mL) canola oil
2 tbsp (30 mL) toasted
   sesame oil

1 tbsp (15 mL) sesame seeds
2 tbsp (30 mL) lemon juice
2 tbsp (30 mL) rice vinegar

1 tsp (5 mL) grated gingerroot
1 tsp (5 mL) grated lemon
   rind

• In jar, shake together canola oil, sesame oil, sesame seeds, lemon juice, vinegar, ginger and
lemon rind. Refrigerate up to 1 month.

Italian Dressing

1/2 cup (125 mL) extra-virgin
   olive oil
2 tbsp (30 mL) balsamic
   vinegar
2 tbsp (30 mL) red wine
   vinegar

1 tbsp (15 mL) Dijon mustard
1 tbsp (15 mL) light
   mayonnaise
1 tsp (5 mL) dried Italian herb
   seasoning (or any combination of basil, oregano,
   thyme leaves)

1 tsp (5 mL) garlic salt
Pepper to taste

• In jar, shake together oil, balsamic vinegar, red wine vinegar, mustard, mayonnaise, herb
seasoning, garlic salt and pepper. Refrigerate up to 1 month.

Mexican Dressing

This recipe is low in fat and is great as a dip for corn chips and for Mexican taco salad.

1/2 cup (125 mL) salsa
2 tbsp (30 mL) red wine
   vinegar

2 tbsp (30 mL) extra-virgin
   olive oil
1 tbsp (15 mL) chopped fresh
   cilantro

1 tsp (5 mL) dried oregano
1 clove garlic, minced

• In jar, shake together salsa, vinegar, oil, cilantro, oregano and garlic. Refrigerate up to 2 weeks.

Quickie Meals from What You've Got

Here are some fast supper-savers and sides from your fridge, freezer and pantry.

PANTRY MEALS AND SIDES

To Make	use	plus	in a	for	to serve with
Garlicky White Beans	19 oz (540 mL) can white kidney beans, drained	1 tbsp (15 mL) olive oil 1 clove garlic, minced 1/4 cup (50 mL) grated Parmesan cheese	skillet	4 min	barbecued chicken, beef or pork
Taco Filling	19 oz (540 mL) can refried beans	1/2 cup (125 mL) salsa	microwave oven (high)	3 min	salad and warmed taco shells
Lentil Soup	19 oz (540 mL) can lentils, drained	14 oz (398 mL) can chicken stock 1 cup (250 mL) frozen corn	pot	5 min	bread and cheese
Chick Pea Salad	19 oz (540 mL) can chick peas, drained	2 tbsp (30 mL) olive oil 2 tbsp (30 mL) lime juice 1 cup (250 mL) chopped fresh parsley Leftover cooked rice	bowl	10 min	barbecued fish or chicken
Pad Thai	1 cup (250 mL) chopped peanuts	1/4 cup (50 mL) peanut sauce 1/4 cup (50 mL) light coconut milk 1/4 cup (50 mL) water 2 cups (500 mL) bean sprouts	pot	5 min	4 cups (1 L) cooked egg noodles

PANTRY SNACKS

To Make	use	plus	in a	for	to serve with
Mexican Tomato Soup	baked corn tortilla chips	28 oz (796 mL) can puréed tomatoes 1 tsp (5 mL) garlic powder 1 tsp (5 mL) dried oregano 1/4 cup (50 mL) grated Parmesan cheese	pot	5 min	crackers and crudités
Brie Crackers	rye crackers	caramelized onions sliced Brie cheese apple slices	broiler	3 min	cocktails
Cream Cheese Bites	rye crackers	cream cheese grated carrots black olives	broiler	2 min	cocktails
Sweet Pecan Topping	2 cups (500 mL) chopped pecans	1/4 cup (50 mL) butter, melted 1/4 cup (50 mL) packed brown sugar	cookie sheet in 400°F (200°C) oven	15 min	over mashed sweet potatoes or ice cream

PANTRY DESSERTS

To Make	use	plus	in a	for
Fruit Cake	1 cup (250 mL) sliced almonds	1 pkg vanilla cake mix 1 cup (250 mL) raisins 1 cup (250 mL) apple sauce 2 apples, sliced	cake pan	as directed
Cherry Trifle	19 oz (540 mL) can cherry pie filling	19 oz (540 mL) can vanilla pudding 3 cups (750 mL) cubed angel food cake	serving bowl	5 min
Pumpkin Pudding	19 oz (540 mL) can pumpkin	2 eggs 1 cup (250 mL) packed brown sugar 1 cup (250 mL) evaporated milk	greased pie plate in 425°F (220°C) oven	1 hour

FREEZER MEALS

To Make	use	plus	in a	for	to serve with
Shrimp Sauté	4 cups (1 L) frozen shrimp, thawed	1 tbsp (15 mL) olive oil 2 cloves garlic, minced 2 cups (500 mL) frozen peas 1/4 cup (50 mL) dried parsley 1 cup (250 mL) chicken stock	skillet	10 min	salad and steamed rice
Seafood Marinara	2 cups (500 mL) frozen shrimp, thawed	18 oz (532 mL) can tomato sauce 1/2 cup (125 mL) grated Parmesan cheese	skillet	8 min	linguine and salad
Curried Scallops	3 cups (750 mL) frozen scallops, thawed	1/4 cup (50 mL) butter 1 tbsp (15 mL) curry powder 1 cup (250 mL) frozen chopped spinach	skillet	10 min	basmati rice
Spicy Puttanesca Sauce	1 cup (250 mL) extra-lean ground beef (thawed in microwave)	1 clove garlic, minced 18 oz (532 mL) can spaghetti sauce 3 tbsp (45 mL) anchovy paste 3 tbsp (45 mL) capers 2 tbsp (30 mL) olive tapenade 1 tsp (5 mL) hot pepper flakes	skillet	20 min	fusilli or spaghetti

FRIDGE MEALS AND SIDES

To Make	use	plus	in a	for	to serve with
Brunch Frittata	6 eggs	any leftover meat or cooked veggies	skillet in oven	20 min	bread and salad
Protein Smoothie	1/2 cup (125 mL) silken tofu	14 oz (398 mL) can chicken stock 1 cup (250 mL) frozen corn	blender	2 min	breakfast
Coleslaw	1 lb (500 g) grated cabbage	1/4 cup (50 mL) light mayonnaise 1 tbsp (15 mL) sugar 2 tbsp (30 mL) vinegar	bowl	2 min	barbecued anything
Stir-fried Cabbage	1 lb (500 g) grated cabbage	1 tbsp (15 mL) toasted sesame oil 1/4 cup (50 mL) soy sauce 1 tbsp (15 mL) grated gingerroot	skillet	5 min	burgers
Chicken Stir-fry	1 lb (500 g) grated cabbage	3 boneless skinless chicken breasts, sliced 1 tbsp (15mL) toasted sesame oil 1/4 cup (50 mL) soy sauce 1 tbsp (15 mL) grated gingerroot	skillet	15 min	steamed rice

FRIDGE DESSERTS

To Make	use	plus	in a	for
Warm Parfait	2 cups (500 mL) vanilla yogurt	3 cups (750 mL) frozen berries	microwave oven (high)	4 min
Fancy Parfait	3 cups (750 mL) suet-free mincemeat	8 vanilla wafers 3 cups frozen yogurt	freezer, layered into 4 martini glasses	1–8 hours

Acknowledgements

No one could have predicted the amount of work necessary for this book to go from a seed of an idea for a business to a tree heavy with fruit. It takes a lot more than water and sunshine, and I owe thanks to a lot of people for their input and support. In utterly random order:

My mumnet group for keeping me alive in the early (and ongoing!) days of mother-hood and for encouraging me, testing recipes (and buying this book!); my mom, Huguette, and her George, my dad, Ron, and my sisters, Michele and Cheryl for thinking I am weird and loving me anyway; my Cape Breton family, who turned out a fine brother-uncle-son and let him marry someone from away; Mercedes Rothwell for her skill in envisioning the prototype; Pam, Jeannie, Monica and Linda for working with me in my "day job" and using these recipes over and over until we got them right; all the clients over the years who trusted us with their tummies; the dieticians and nutri-tionists who trusted us with their clients, especially Barbie Casselman and Aileen Burford-Mason; Kirsten Hanson, who got an unsolicited prototype from an unknown and took a chance—you made me an author, thank you; the entire team at HarperCollins, who made me feel welcome and worthy; Hal Roth, Rosemarie Superville and Paolo Cristante, who made the days in the photo studio fun and beautiful.

To Donna Beck, Erin Booth, Mary Delli-Colli and Babs Thurber, thanks for being awesome friends and "other moms" when I just could not be there for Jameson; the Keilhauers, the Viscas and the Bedards for being "chosen family"; the Asplers, the Burnses, the Wilsons, the Robbs and the Nemetts for being superb supporters and darned good party guests; Jackie Dais-Visca and Fiona Orr, who receive the award for best legal interpreters when reams of legalese make no sense; recipe testers, we all owe a lot to you; and all of the cooking class kids who try everything, teach me something every day and have learned to say "It's not my taste" instead of "Ewwww."

I owe the most thanks to my little family: my husband, Guy Ratchford, who saw the train coming and chose not to get off the tracks; he actually got on board my locomo-tive life and became the fuel that keeps me going. My daughter, Jameson, has been the impetus for everything: her birth set me on a path of motherhood, causing a career veer that led to this book. Trying to balance work and home may never have happened if not for her. She teaches me to be patient, kind, humble and real—but she still has to eat her broccoli.

Index

Recipe titles in italics are "Grab and Go" items made with leftovers from other recipes.